CALLED BY PROPHECY – LED BY EXPERIENCE

Henry and Carol Jacobs

CALLED BY PROPHECY
LED BY EXPERIENCE
VOLUME ONE

A Personal Journey With GOD
and A Modern-Day Prophet

Published 2017
by Henry and Carol Jacobs

ISBN 978-0-473-39650-3

© Copyright Henry and Carol Jacobs 2017
All rights reserved.

Except for the purpose of fair reviewing, no part of this publication may be reproduced or transmitted in any form or by any means, electronic or mechanical, including photocopying, recording or any information storage and retrieval system, without prior written permission from the publisher.

Printed by The Copy Press, Nelson, New Zealand. www.copypress.co.nz

When God says it - That settles it
'Believe in the Lord your God and you shall be established, believe His prophets and you shall prosper'
(2 Chronicles 20:20) (NKJV)

Contents

Foreword One		xiii
Foreword Two		xv
Foreword Three		xvii
Endorsements		xxi
Dedication		xxiii
Prologue		xxv
	Introduction	1
	AUTHOR: HENRY JACOBS	1
	CO-AUTHOR: CAROL JACOBS	7
Chapter One	**Overview: What Is Prophecy?**	11
	THE PROPHETIC WORD OF GOD	11
	THE SOURCE OF PROPHECY	14
	THE PURPOSES OF PROPHECY	17
Chapter Two	**The Process of Prophecy**	20
	PROPHETIC REVELATION	20
	THE HEART OF GOD	22
	FULFILLING AND RESTORING GOD'S PLAN	25
	ISAIAH, A MAJOR PROPHET	27
Chapter Three	**Our Journey and Calling Begin**	32
	HIGH SCHOOL YEARS: 1981 TO 1985	32

	Discovering My Purpose: 1986 To 1990	35
	Our Relationship Is Tested: 1991	40
Chapter Four	**Overcoming Challenges**	51
	Marriage And A Promotion: 1992	51
	Finding A New Home: 1993	62
Chapter Five	**Serving God and The Community**	67
	'Youth Aflame' And Community Achievements	67
	Family Reconciliation	71
	Working With Special Interest Groups	73
Chapter Six	**Wider Opportunities**	75
	When One Door Closes ...	75
	... Another Door Opens	83
	Matters Go Awry	86
	An Unintended Ministry	92
	In The Belly Of The Whale	99
Chapter Seven	**Back Home Again**	107
	A Slow Start	107
	Rewards For Faithful Service	115
	Setting Off Again	122
Chapter Eight	**New Country, New Challenges**	127
	Mighty Oaks From Little Acorns	127
	Mixed Blessings	131
	Mentoring And Co-Founding A Church	138
Chapter Nine	**The Role of The Prophet and Its Impact**	146
	The Importance Of The Prophet	146
	Heed The Word Of Prophecy	151
Chapter Ten	**Understanding the Process of Our Journey**	158
	How Do We Receive Prophecy?	158
	What Do We Do While We Wait On God To Fulfil Our Prophecy?	162

	ATTACKS TO KILL THE PROPHECY	164
	STAND STRONG IN YOUR FAITH: DURING THE BATTLE AND THE ATTACKS	166
Chapter Eleven	**Conclusion**	173
	Epilogue	177
	YOUTH AFLAME INTERNATIONAL	177
	H.P. JAKES MINISTRIES	178
	Biography	181
	HENRY	181
	CAROL	182

Prophecy is about believing in a spoken word from God even when everything else seems unbelievable. It encompasses —

The inspired declaration of His divine will and purpose, and

A prediction of something to come.

Foreword One

Pastor Emeritus *Lourens J. Maralack, Apostolic Faith Mission (AFM) of South Africa, Boland Regional executive member and retired senior pastor of the Paarl Assembly.*

It affords me great pleasure to recommend this practical book *Called by Prophecy - Led by Experience* authored by one of my spiritual sons, Henry, and his wife, Carol. Henry is an ex-youth leader of the Apostolic Faith Mission Church, a church which I pastored for close on forty years.

I have known Henry for many years, and during this period he has been an absolute blessing to the youth ministry and to our congregation as a whole. Henry accepted the Lord as his personal Saviour at the tender age of twelve.

Up to this point in his life, Henry has been to the proverbial 'hell and back' and has lived to tell the story. He and his wife were sorely tried and tested but, through the grace of God, he emerged strong in faith. He suffered great hardship in Apartheid South Africa and then, even when they left the shores of this country, he was innocently incarcerated in the USA and deported back to

South Africa. He did not surrender; and now lives and works in New Zealand as a pastor.

The book covers the experience of receiving and responding to personal prophecy, the journey of the authors and their eventual calling.

This book is a result of an utterance of God that came to the authors on 30 December 2004 whilst in the USA, to the effect that they should document everything they have gone through in their lives. This utterance was confirmed by Sister Dicks who called them on 3 January 2006, and said that while she was in prayer she saw the book in her spirit during a vision, and spurred them on to record their experiences. Ten years later the book is a reality.

I am glad, as an eighty-four-year-old Pastor Emeritus, to have the privilege of endorsing this book on prophecy. The authors have researched the subject for a lengthy period of time and, in fact, are a product of this phenomenon. In the book, Henry and his wife speak with authority on prophecy and substantiate it with appropriate Scriptures from the Bible.

This book will give the reader a thorough, practical and inspirational understanding of the gift of prophecy. It is meant for anyone who wants to sojourn with the authors on their spiritual journey and share the experience of how prophecy manifested in their lives.

30 January 2017

Foreword Two

Pastor Dr Daniel Andrew (Ph.D.), Apostolic Faith Mission of South Africa (Apostoliese Geloofsending van Suid Afrika), Pastor at Rosenhof - AFM Moorreesburg, South Africa.

When you read the title of this book, *Called by Prophecy - Led by Experience*, you do not really understand just how fully it relates to the personal journey of Henry, Carol and their daughter, Candice, in three countries.

In this first volume of their personal life story, the Jacobs family narrates how prophecies 'spoken over' their lives became reality. What is quite astonishing is the role of Sister Jackie Dicks, the mouthpiece of God in their lives, who guided them through some of the most life changing experiences over more than three decades.

The foundation of the Church is built on the apostles and the prophets, and in this book a great deal of very well balanced research is presented on the importance of prophecy today. Their strong focus on the experience of personal prophecy in the life of the believer and its fulfilment, gives the narrative a legitimacy that is unquestioned.

I would like to congratulate Henry, Carol and Candice for their courage and willingness to obey the voice of God in their lives. The sharing of deep personal stories of trauma and injustice can bring hope to persons and nations who are still trapped in the past.

May this first volume bring hope to those who have given up and accepted negative and degrading circumstances as being beyond restoration and without hope of reconciliation.

May the Lord raise more women and men that can hear the voice of God clearly and speak it without fear or favour.

Foreword Three

Pastor Eben J.P. Mourries BA.Theol. (Stell.), M.Theol. (Stell.), Ph.D.Theol. (Stell.). Senior Pastor, Breakthru Restoration Community Church, Wellington, South Africa.

Upon reading the manuscript *Called by Prophecy - Led by Experience*, the Holy Spirit impressed upon my heart Ephesians 4:11-12, 'It was He who gave some to be apostles, some to be prophets, some to be evangelists, and some to be pastors and teachers; to prepare God's people for works of service, so that the body of Christ's may be built up' (NIV).[1]

The personal journey of prophecy, and positive and negative experiences which Henry and Carol Jacobs and their daughter, Candice, went through was God's way to prepare them for 'their works of service' in the body of Christ in different countries and on a global scale. Their personal prophecies shall come into fulfilment as they stay obedient to His Word and to their calling.

---

[1] This quote and subsequent ones in Foreword 3 are all from the New International Version of the Bible.

When I read through this book their experiences reminded me of the journey of Joseph, starting from Genesis 37, when Joseph received his dreams, until Genesis 50, when Joseph died at the age of a hundred and ten. In Genesis 45:5, Joseph uttered these profound words, 'And now, do not be distressed and do not be angry with yourselves for selling me here, because it was to save lives that God sent me ahead of you' (NIV).

Against this background, it is my joy to write the foreword to this vital book on the subject of prophecy and its impact on our lives, and to be a spiritual mentor to such a man and woman of God who have diligently pursued the calling and will of God regardless of the sacrifices required.

Henry and Carol wrote this book from the heart. They went through personal experiences of prophecy and, in some instances, I was part of their journey of prophecy and experience. My first encounter with Henry was between August and September 1996, in Wellington, South Africa, when I was appointed as the associate pastor of the Wellington Assemblies of God Church and he was the community liaison officer of the South African Police Service in the district.

Jointly, the two of us would organise crime prevention programmes for youth at risk, as well as programmes to keep the school children busy during the school holidays. Since those early days, Henry had a passion for God and a desire to make a difference in the lives of ordinary people and communities through the Gospel of Jesus Christ. He was also the founder of Youth Aflame, and the Boland Music Festival, which draws together hundreds of young people from different churches, youth groups and communities for fellowship and life-skills training.

In November 2000, I was invited, as a foreign delegate, together with my senior pastor, the late Pastor J.D. April, to attend the National Convocation of the Church of God in Christ (COGIC) in Memphis, Tennessee, USA; an event that attracted more than 70,000 people. Henry and Carol Jacobs had a catering business at that stage, and they offered to hold a fundraising dinner to help cover the cost of my trip overseas — including spending money.

In 2001, he was youth pastor in Zion Fellowship Church of God in Christ, while I was the associate pastor in the same church, and we had wonderful times in the ministry together.

During May and June 2003, knowing that Henry and Carol were about to leave for the United States, my wife and I approached them with an offer to rent their house for a year with the first option to buy it, should it be put up for sale. To our amazement they told us they had had a dream about the selling of their house, which served as a prophecy that they would rent the house out for a short period of time, and then sell it to a pastor's family with a young child. When we came to them with the offer to rent and not buy, they felt that the prophecy was confirmed by God in that it should be us they select as tenants. We only rented the house for three months before we applied for a mortgage bond which was quickly approved. We stayed in that house, 46 Conrad Street, Mountain View, Paarl, for more than seven blessed years, just because of the faithfulness of God and Henry and Carol's sensitivity and obedience to God.

Henry and Carol Jacobs know what they are talking about when they speak of heartache, trials, and pain from the past, but they did not allow the enemy to stop them from pursuing the call of God for them to dedicate their lives to His service. Henry and Carol have a message burning in their hearts. It's a message of hope. It's a message of encouragement. It's a message that many people need to hear because many people wonder for a long time about what God is going to do with their lives.

After more than twenty years in ministry, my wife and I and our two daughters are very grateful for the friendship we have enjoyed with Henry, Carol and Candice Jacobs, and that we have been part of their personal journey with God and a prophet, Sister Jackie. The Word of God in Job 42:12 will be true in their lives, 'The Lord blessed the latter part of Job's life more than the former part' (NIV).[2]

---

[2] The New International Version of the Bible.

Endorsements

Pastor Pano Paulo, Masterton Samoan Assembly of God, New Zealand.

Pastor Henry and Carol Jacobs are trusted friends of mine since we first met. For over four years we enjoyed a close association, and Henry Jacobs proved himself to be a man of perceptive thought with a wide knowledge of social, national, international and biblical issues. His passion in serving God and others in the ministry was always stimulating and challenging, and he had the ability to strike at the heart of vital subjects.

Henry Jacobs is a man of passion and even in times of trouble he takes appropriate action and keeps on moving forward, as the apostle Paul urged, 'Be ready in season and out of season' (2 Timothy 4:2)(NKJV).[3]

We are all children of the Almighty God and inseparable from Him in whom we live and move and have our being. God is Spirit, omnipresent and omnipotent, and when uplifted in consciousness we realize our oneness with Him.

---

[3] New King James Version of the Bible.

'For the eyes of the Lord run to and fro throughout the whole earth to show Himself strong on behalf of those whose heart is loyal to Him' (2 Chronicles 16:9) (NKJV).

Henry Jacobs is one of those persons, exactly — whose heart is loyal to Him. My wife, Meipo, and I are grateful to have him and his wife Carol as true friends of ours in our ministry in the Wairarapa, New Zealand. I am sure you will be inspired when you read their book *Called by Prophecy - Led by Experience*.

* * *

Pastor Louis Witbooi, Koinonia Christian Fellowship, New Zealand.

The authors humbly share their personal prophetic experiences in this book, and by doing so they shed light on how prophecy can direct one's journey. The aim of prophecy is to increase faith in God and bring about change and repentance. May you be inspired by their journey and take God on His Word.

Dedication

This book is dedicated to:

Sister Jackie Dicks – The Prophet of God, who never diverted from her mission in hearing God correctly or wavered in her faith, so as to convey the messages exactly as given to her by God, like the Prophet Samuel did in the Old Testament.

Sister Jackie Dicks, December 2016 in South Africa
Photograph taken by her daughter

The late Mrs Magdalene Daniels – Carol's mother, who dedicated her life to ensuring that her children received Jesus Christ as Lord and Saviour, and provided for them. She was known as 'Ma Palmy'.

'Ma Palmy', 2002 in South Africa
Photograph taken by Henry Jacobs

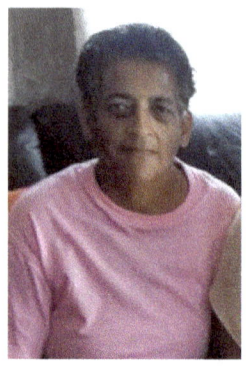

Mrs Margaret Jacobs – Henry's mother, who endured beatings and abuse, yet continued providing strength and love to her seven children. She never lost faith and her strength carried them through difficulties.

Margaret Jacobs, Mother's Day 2004 in South Africa
Photograph taken by Henry Jacobs

Candice-carne Joy Jacobs – daughter and inspiration to the journey travelled. Her faith and love for God is inspiring.

Photograph taken by Henry Jacobs, 2012

Our families, who believed in us and who were very supportive in all our travels; they were always praying for us. Without them this book would not be possible.

Prologue

Our strong Christian faith and the brutal, oppressive Apartheid era in South Africa form the context in which this book is set. This is due to Apartheid's pervasive presence in our daily lives before 1990, and the wide reaching effects of its aftermath in the post-Apartheid years. The enormous influence it had on almost every aspect of our childhood and early adulthood is second only to that of our belief in God and our Christian way of life. The Apartheid regime in South Africa to a great extent, shaped our lives and those of our parents, grandparents and ancestors as far back as we can recall. For those readers — perhaps the younger ones, who are not fully aware of the key features of Apartheid, we have provided a brief overview but do encourage you to investigate the subject further.

Apartheid, which in English translates as 'separateness' was a system of institutionalised laws and policies of segregation and discrimination on grounds of race, that was established in South Africa in 1948 by the National Party which governed the country until 1994. Although the policy of Apartheid began officially in 1948, the practice of racial discrimination, in fact, has deep roots in South African society, dating back to the late 18th century.

Apartheid was based on an ideology of white supremacy and its basic premise was that the races must be kept separated and allowed to develop in their own way – in reality it was a system designed to keep white South Africans in control of the country.

A few of the major points in the timeline of Apartheid are:

- The Prohibition of Mixed Marriages Act of 1949, which outlawed marriage between Europeans (whites) and non-Europeans (non-whites). The following year new legislation banned sexual intercourse between Europeans and non-Europeans.

- The Population Registration Act of 1950, which provided the basic framework for apartheid by classifying all South Africans by race (largely determined by physical features), including Bantu (black Africans), Coloured (mixed race) and white. A fourth category, Asian (meaning Indian and Pakistani) was later added. In some cases, the legislation split families; parents could be classified as white, while their children were classified as coloured.

- The Group Areas Act of 1950, however, was the core of apartheid in South Africa. The act marked off areas of land for different racial groups, and made it illegal for people to live in any but their designated areas.

- The Black (Natives) Laws Amendment Act of 1952 amended the 1945 Native Urban Areas Consolidation Act, stipulating that all black people over the age of sixteen years were required to carry passes, and that no black person could stay in an urban area more than 72 hours unless allowed to by Section 10.

- The Native Labour Act in 1953 placed more restrictions on the black majority in South Africa. The effect of the law was to prohibit strike action by blacks.

- The General Laws Amendment Act of 1964 (passed in 1963) or the 90-Day Act, provided for any person to be detained in jail, without trial, for ninety days. Further, on the expiration of such, the person could be re-arrested under the same law for another ninety days, a process this law allowed to be repeated indefinitely.

Other key features of the Apartheid regime included:

- The fact that for years the system was supported theologically by a perversion of the Calvinist doctrine of predestination held in the South African Dutch Reformed Church of which the majority of the leading white political leaders were members.

- Only the white South Africans and none of the other races were considered full citizens, even though they and their ancestors had been born in the country.

- Access to jobs; community facilities; all forms and levels of education; medical, health and social services; public transport; financial services; business ownership; housing; sport, entertainment, leisure and recreational facilities – and much, much more were all determined by one's racial classification.

Despite strong and consistent violent and non-violent opposition to Apartheid both within South Africa by the majority black population and other 'enlightened' or liberal South Africans of all racial groups, and outside of South Africa in the form of ostracization, boycotts and economic sanctions; its laws and policies remained in effect for almost fifty years.

In 1990, Nelson Mandela was released from prison after a period of twenty-seven years and began to negotiate a peaceful end to Apartheid and a transition to a democracy in South Africa. In 1991, the government of President F.W. de Klerk began to repeal most of the legislation that provided the basis for Apartheid.

Apartheid formally ended in 1994 with the first 'free' election which allowed the participation of all adult voters, irrespective of racial group. With that election Nelson Mandela became the first black president of South Africa. The expectation was that things would change for the better.

South Africa's Truth and Reconciliation Commission was set up under the 1995 Promotion of National Unity and Reconciliation Act, to investigate crimes committed during the Apartheid era.

The introduction of this Commission brought healing to many black South Africans. Victims of abuse and torture at the hands of the 'white' government could finally find closure to their pain. But in contrast, many people saw this process as a way of opening old wounds. Nelson Mandela had great intentions in reconciling the nation but there were those who wanted the white people to pay for the pain and suffering caused by the Apartheid era.

It was even more hurtful for us who grew up as coloured people during this time of transition in the 1990s. For us, jobs became more and more scare as most black people felt a sense of entitlement to good, well-paying jobs. Many white people were demoted and dismissed from their employment to make room for black people, even if this was at the expense of losing qualified and experienced employees.

It is estimated that since 1995, more than 60% of coloured people in Cape Town find it hard to secure employment due to jobs being reserved for black people.

Today we see the unemployment rate in South Africa at an all-time high. Young people are finding it difficult to get a job after completing high school. Professional young people find it even harder to secure well-paying jobs due to political party infighting and manipulation. There is a tendency among political parties to see which of their members can become wealthy very quickly by using their authority and privilege, often in unethical and even corrupt ways. Those in power are also inclined to take care of their own family and friends instead of the citizens of the country. It almost feels like we are experiencing a form of 'reverse Apartheid', where blacks implement laws and regulations to benefit themselves, leaving the whites and coloureds to fend for themselves as best they can.

Introduction

AUTHOR: HENRY JACOBS

I was born in February 1967, in the Western Cape province of South Africa, and was raised in a household of five boys and two girls. I am the eldest of a set of twins and my twin brother is Abraham Isaac Jacobs. My parents were devoted Christians with the Church of the Nazarene in Hanover Park, Cape Flats, Cape Town. I remember my dad being the church elder and Sunday school teacher, and my mom carrying us off to church every Sunday. We grew up very poor, not having food every night, and electricity was considered a luxury. I recall going to bed many times having eaten only one slice of bread sprinkled with sugar. Mom and Dad did their very best to raise us in a godly home. They were employed full-time, and Trevor, my eldest brother, ran the household – cleaning and cooking. When Trevor started working, I had to take over the household responsibilities as our parents expected that the house be clean and the food cooked when they arrived home at the end of the day.

Growing up during the Apartheid years was tough on us as

children because we were 'classified' by the government as being non-white South Africans. We were not allowed to attend any school other than a so-called coloured school in the Cape Flats, where the Afrikaans language was forced on us. We were compelled by law to stick to our racial groups and their designated residential areas as prescribed by the government. I remember when South Africa had the major youth uprising in 1976, being about nine years old at the time. I recall being part of the community throwing stones at the police and demonstrating on the streets of Hanover Park. Even though I was so young at the time, I knew that 1976 was a bloody year. The experience had a major impact on my life, and I started to show signs of having an interest in politics.

In 1979, our family moved from Hanover Park to Mitchells Plain, where my life took a drastic turn. I was about twelve years old when I was sexually molested by a family member, an uncle, and that incident traumatised me. When this abuse occurred, I did not understand the extent and nature of the effect it had on me because I did not know any better, and felt bad about what had happened. My mother was not aware of what was going on, and at the time she had a lot to cope with in her own life, having to deal with my father who was hardly ever at home. I was always afraid to be around my uncle whenever the family would visit.

My dad and mom withdrew from church life after we moved to Mitchells Plain. My dad became a very angry and abusive person. Until then he had been a very good man, but started drinking and hanging out with his drinking companions. He went through a season in his life where matters got out of hand. My dad would give us beatings for any negative thing like not doing well at school, misbehaving and fighting with one another. He would hit my mother, and many days were torment for me as a child. He started having extra-marital affairs with various women, and that was a turning point in my parents' marriage. I do not recall seeing my dad drunk or out of control in public, but I do believe that alcohol played a role in his change in behaviour. Dad would try to keep his 'secret life' hidden, but Mom had a way of just knowing when something was wrong. Mom would take the kids and follow Dad when he went out at night to his 'girls', and when he returned he would beat my mother. We were afraid of what he had become. He would find fault with Mom's cooking and throw the food against the wall to show his dissatisfaction.

It got to a point where, on one occasion, he locked us in a room and turned on an LPG gas tank with the intention of setting us on fire. There we were, seven kids and our mom, locked in a room with windows that were secured by cast iron burglar bars, and there was no way to escape. I managed to get out by forcing my head through a small opening in the bars and sought help from the neighbours. The police said we were lucky to get out in time as the gas had already filled the room, and were fortunate that none of us were hurt.

That was the turning point for us as a family because we, the five brothers, then decided it was time to protect our mother and sisters. One evening we, as his sons, took matters into our own hands and defended our sisters and mother against our father. Dad was shocked by us going that far but he changed after this experience. I suppose he never thought we would take such extreme measures. One thing we always knew, though, was that Dad and Mom loved us no matter the difficulties we went through as a family. Dad would always show his love by doing things for us. He was a very good father except for the unnecessary beatings we had to endure at his hands.

Things started to change after the time when we stood up to him to protect our mother. Dad became more of a distant, withdrawn father to us, and it was not long after this that Mom decided to get divorced from him. I remember when I was at high school, how Mom would do any type of work in the factory to be able to take care of us. She would 'break her back' so that we could attend and finish school. Dad finally left us to move in with another woman who is now his wife. Dad eventually recommitted his life to Christ in 2010, and Mom returned to church life after 2000.

Salvation

I came to accept Jesus Christ as Lord and Saviour at the age of twelve, in 1979, whilst attending an evening service at an Anglican Church. The preacher was asking the question, "Where will you spend eternity if you should die tonight?" The Scripture was from John 3:3, 'Except a man be born again, he cannot see the Kingdom of God' (KJV).[4] I jumped at the opportunity to know Jesus.

Over the following years from 1979 to 1986, I was very involved in church life, being a Church Lads' Brigade member, altar boy, youth group leader, and Sunday school teacher with Christ the Mediator Anglican Church, Portlands, Mitchells Plain. The year 1979 was a good one. While my mom and dad did their best to raise us in the Church, they did not attend church services often. They were and still are good parents.

---

[4] King James Version of the Bible.

We had very little to eat at home and shoes were a blessing due to our large family size. In 1980, at the age of thirteen I started working at the supermarket during the school holidays, and that allowed me to pay my way through high school. I bought my first pair of shoes when I was fourteen years old. During my high school career the principal asked me to lead the school assembly on Monday mornings. This meant that I read from Scripture and lead the entire school in prayer. I was groomed by God to be a leader and a preacher.

This opportunity at high school earned me the reputation of being a 'preacher', and I was also recognised as being a student leader. Growing up during the Apartheid years in South Africa meant that I faced many challenges. We grew up in poverty and gang violence was almost a daily occurrence. I became involved in the political environment and was soon the chairman of the Mitchells Plain branch of COSAS (Congress of South African Students).[5] These were troubled years for us as teenagers, growing up in an era when you were not allowed to interact with, or even be in the same vicinity as a white person.

When I finally left school, I thought that it would be better to fight the enemy from within, and I joined the South African Navy. My time as a chef in the Navy too, was not without trouble. On one occasion, I was travelling from Simon's Town (home to the South African Navy) to Cape Town by train. I was dressed in my white

---

[5] The Congress of South African Students (COSAS) was established in June 1979 as a national organisation to represent the interests of Black school students in the wake of the Soweto uprisings. By the time of its banning in 1985, it was estimated that the organisation enjoyed the support of almost three million students, or more than half the country's Black students. (http://www.sahistory.org.za/topic/congress-south-african-students-cosas)

naval uniform and seated in a carriage reserved for 'whites only'. Next to me sat a white female and we were secretly talking and cracking some laughs. The train stopped at a station and two white police officers boarded. They cursed me, using degrading language, calling me a 'hotnot' (an offensive, vulgar word akin to 'nigger' in the USA). I felt embarrassed; I mean, here I am serving the 'white Apartheid government' of the day, and I get treated like this? They grabbed me, kicked me to the ground, and by the time the train arrived at the next station, I was covered in blood and hurting. They threw me out of the train at the station, handcuffed me, and said in Afrikaans, "Dit is wat jy kry as jy nie jou plek ken nie." ("This is what you get if you don't know your place.") Later they told me that I was going to spend the night sleeping with the dogs in the police cells just for being in the company of a white girl. This was an experience that I will never forget because it was the core of what the Apartheid regime represented: being targeted because of the colour of one's skin.

The main reason for me joining the Navy was to set an example and make a positive impact on the youth in our community, by showing them that if we want things to change, we need to be the agents of change by becoming involved. I was tired of wanting things to get better, and I knew I had to do something about it. Accepting the Lord as my Saviour at a young age was the turning point in my life and the start of a journey with God, experiencing His awesome power and divine work in my life. The lyrics 'He who began a good work in you will be faithful to complete it',[6] come to mind.

---

[6] Song/Hymn: 'He who began a good work in you', words and music by Jon Mohr, for the Steve Green Ministries. © 1988 Birdwing Music/Jonathan Mark Music.

Co-Author: Carol Jacobs

From the time I was a young girl, I have always been in the house of the Lord. My upbringing was somewhat integrated with church life. My mother was a strong believer in God and that encouraged a constant desire in me for more of God. For this I am so thankful, to have a mother who had a strong faith in God. I come from a close-knit family, one in which we received lots of love. My parents were strong believers in getting ahead and prospering in life and always encouraged us to do our best. My mother was a nurse for almost all her life, and my dad was a hard worker and a good provider for the family. I was saved at a young age and it was my mother whose faith in God made me long for more and more of Him. My dad came to the knowledge of salvation late in his years. Praise be to God. I could never have known that my desire for God would flourish through a prophetic word being spoken over my life. At the time this prophetic incident occurred I did not understand it, being immature and young in my relationship with the Lord, and not understanding salvation as I do now.

During that period in my life I was fired up for God and always active in the youth ministry. I am sure you know what I am talking about — those strong emotions experienced when you first give your heart to God. You would not stop for anything that tried to hinder you in preaching and testifying about God's goodness. Yes, I was one of those who at a young age were 'hungry' for the presence of God. Our youth would get together and have prayer nights seeking the face of God and would not mind spending time in God's presence. For me, it was always a joy being in the presence of the Lord.

Our church's youth arranged combined youth services during which we would join up with other youth groups doing outreach work. This, combined with our hospital visitations, was always on our list for winning souls for Christ.

Well, this overview so far is mainly about my young life of ministry before I met Henry, who became my husband. At the time I met Henry, I was studying to be a teacher. Our relationship grew as we grew in Christ together, working with the youth in our church congregation and doing ministry at our local church. After we got engaged in August 1991, Henry and I would do hospital visitations on Sunday afternoons, engage in outreach youth events on Saturdays, arrange open-air services and do youth work together. I was teaching at the Alpha School for Autistic Children at that time. We never knew then that it was actually the start of our journey with God and walking in faith with God through the power of prophecy.

We had prayer groups within our church which met weekly to attend to prayer requests submitted by the congregation. In 1990, a lady at our local church, Sister Fredericks, who was part of the prayer group, came to talk to me and Henry after a church service. It was during the time when we were still courting and enjoying ministry life for Christ.

By her approach she seemed quite desperate to talk to us. Not knowing what it was all about, we eagerly stepped aside from the rest of the prayer group to hear what she had to say. At this moment, filled with great curiosity, Henry and I looked at each other. And then we found that we were being exposed to a word from God. Sister Fredericks mentioned that a prophet, Sister Jackie, would like to talk to us because she had been prompted by the Holy Spirit to pray for us, and that we needed to visit her urgently.

By this stage we had become anxious about the reason for the meeting and the topic that would be discussed. Still being immature in our walk with God, we acknowledged the request and quite politely agreed that we would go and see Sister Jackie. We arranged a date and time when we would get together and Sister Fredericks agreed to introduce us to her as this would be our first meeting.

We always believed, and were taught back then, that when a prophet speaks a word over your life, you need to obey and believe God's intention or message in that spoken word. At that time, Henry and I were about twenty-five years old and did not understand 'the prophetic word'. Yes, we were saved, and loved the Lord and what God was doing in and through us, but we did not understand any other spiritual dimension of being a child of God.

Then the time arrived for us to meet Sister Jackie. It was a beautiful Monday evening when we stood on her porch, gently knocking on her front door, not knowing what to expect. The door opened and that was the first time we met her. Coming face to face with a prophet and, on top of that, one who requested our presence, meant serious business to us at the time. Feeling both anxious and excited, we simply stood there on her porch. She kindly invited us in and humbly introduced herself. As we sat with her she modestly explained what her ministry was all about, and quietly shared with us how God had been using her in prophetic ministry. I suppose she could tell that we were not knowledgeable about prophecy and prophesying, and did not have much understanding of it. She allowed us to share a bit about our lives and how God was using us in ministry. Then she began praying for us, and what an awesome time we had in the presence of the Lord! We understood then that our journey is our process, not our destiny.

Chapter One

Overview: What Is Prophecy?

THE PROPHETIC WORD OF GOD

This concept is comprehensively covered in Harvestime International Network's[7] prophecy course material's *Introduction Section*, in the article *The Prophetic Word of God*,[8] (2010):

> The word 'prophecy' means to speak forth. Bible prophecy includes three basic kinds of speaking forth:
> 1. A message of inspiration from God.
> 2. Prediction of future events in God's eternal plan.
> 3. An interpretation for man of the acts of God.

---

[7] Harvestime International Network is a non-denominational Christian organisation. www.harvestime.org.
[8] Online course material: *Introductory Section: The Prophetic Word of God*, 2010, p.1. Presented online through their Go-In-Faith educational service. URL: http://goinfaith.weebly.com/uploads/4/6/4/2/4642437/prophecycourse_introduction.pdf

God commissioned each prophet of the Bible to fulfil a particular role in His plan —
1. As interpreters they explained God's acts to men.
2. As spokesmen they voiced God's truth. They spoke messages of hope and inspiration.
3. As prophets they predicted future events in God's plan through revelation given by the Holy Spirit. The predictions of Bible prophecy are beyond the power of human ability. They include a sufficient number of details to eliminate speculation or guessing.

The method most often used was the spoken word. God would tell the prophet the words to speak. For example, God said to the prophet Jeremiah: 'for thou shalt go to all that I shall send thee, and whatsoever I command thee thou shalt speak' (Jeremiah 1:7) (KJV).[9]

The following Scripture is relevant too: 'Before I formed you in the womb I knew you, and before you were born I consecrated you; I appointed you a prophet to the nations' (Jeremiah 1:5) (ESV).[10]

Being called by God and chosen for a purpose is an amazing journey, one filled with exciting experiences that give your life meaning. The journey, though, does come with positive and negative challenges.

Carol and I started out as just an ordinary couple but have evolved into a purposeful couple on a divine mission for Christ. We were prayed for, prophesied over, and given a word of wisdom — all of which has resulted in this book.

---

[9] The King James Version of the Bible.
[10] English Standard Version of the Bible.

Our journey is filled with not only the good and positive aspects of serving God, but also the trials and difficulties that come with it. While we experienced the mountain highs of life, it was in the valley lows that we could see God's hand upon our lives. It is in these experiences that we could know God and trust in Him. We are human and are tempted daily. Being called and chosen by God does not make us immune to any attacks by Satan, in fact, we become a greater target for attacks. Yes, the greater the trial, the greater the victory. God promises in His Word that He will never leave us nor forsake us. He will be our refuge and fortress in time of need.

Every time we were given a prophecy by Sister Jackie Dicks, those prophecies came to fulfilment. Everything that was spoken through Sister Jackie happened at the exact time and dates predicted. The confirmations of the prophecies she spoke were real and manifested in other people we came across on this journey.

For us this journey has purpose, whether it is to inspire, empower or motivate. God spoke to us on 30 December 2004 in the USA, telling us to document everything that God would take us through on our journey. This was confirmed when Sister Jackie Dicks called us from South Africa on 3 January 2006, and said that while praying she saw a vision in her spirit of a book that we had written, and that we should keep a record of what we experience in our relationship and journey with God.

We obeyed and now more than ten years later, God has made it possible for us to do just that.

Our prayers are that this book will encourage, inspire and motivate readers to obey God at all cost, to develop a sincere desire to do the will of God, and never neglect prophecy or a true word spoken over their lives. Make sure you test such a spoken word by the Word of God and a confirmation for yourself. When someone prophesies over you or gives you a word from God, keep that word at the centre of your prayers so that you receive confirmation through prayer, from God's spirit. You may also find that as you search for the confirmation you need, someone comes to you and tells you something that confirms what was said in prophecy. The Holy Spirit is faithful and will confirm such a word received through prophecy.

The Scripture that would be very pertinent to us throughout the entire journey is, 'Believe in the Lord your God, and you shall be established; believe His prophets, and you shall prosper' (2 Chronicles 2:20) (NKJV).[11]

The continuation of the journey is what makes writing about it interesting, since it never comes to an end. Any journey has potholes along its path, and it's how we navigate around the potholes that separate us from others. Potholes are those areas in your life which always go unseen and are hidden. They are the dark side of your life that involves the very real inner struggles with weaknesses and shortcomings that have to be addressed.

We are all in need of redemption, forgiveness and salvation. We are weak in our own strength and need the strength of the Lord Jesus Christ.

THE SOURCE OF PROPHECY

The Holy Spirit is the only true source of prophecy. We must look at all prophecies and prophetic utterances in light of the Word of

---

[11] The New King James Version of the Bible.

God. Prophecy that is truly from God will never override or be in conflict with Scripture. Genuine prophecy will always align with Scripture.

Harvestime International Network's article *The Prophetic Word of God*,[12] (2010), provides the following insight about the source of prophecy:

> The source of Biblical prophecy is God who reveals His message to man through the Holy Spirit:
>
> 'For the prophecy came not in old time by the will of man; but holy men of God spake as they were moved by the Holy Ghost' (2 Peter 1:21) (KJV).[13]
>
> 'But God hath revealed them unto us by His Spirit: for the Spirit searcheth all things, yea, the deep things of God' (1 Corinthians 2:10).
>
> God can speak accurately of the future because:
>
> 'Known unto God are all His works from the beginning of the world' (Acts 15:18).
>
> 'Remember the former things of old: For I am God, and there is none else; I am God, and there is none like me' (Isaiah 46:9).

---

[12] Ibid, pp. 2-3.
[13] In this section all scripture quotation are from the King James Version of the Bible unless stated otherwise.

'Declaring the end from the beginning, and from ancient times the things that are not yet done, saying, My counsel shall stand, and I will do all my pleasure' (Isaiah 46: 10).

God raises up true prophets:

'The Lord thy God will raise up unto thee a Prophet from the midst of thee, of thy brethren, like unto me; unto him ye shall hearken' (Deuteronomy 18:15).

God reveals His future plans to these prophets so they can prepare His people for the future:

'Surely the Lord God will do nothing but He revealeth His secret unto His servants the prophets' (Amos 3:7).

Satan imitates true prophecy through false predictions by fortune tellers, witches, and astrologers. These methods are not of God. The Prophet Daniel said:

'...The secret which the king hath demanded cannot the wise men, the astrologers, the magicians, the soothsayers shew unto the king,

'But there is a God in heaven that revealeth secrets, and maketh known to the king Nebuchadnezzar what shall be in the latter days...' (Daniel 2: 27-28).

True prophecy directs attention to Jesus Christ:

'Wherefore I give you to understand, that no man speaking by the Spirit of God calleth Jesus accursed; and that no man can say that Jesus is the Lord, but by the Holy Ghost' (I Corinthians 12:3).

The Bible warns of false prophets (Matthew 24:11, 24; Mark 13:22). A person called 'the False Prophet' will be evident in events at the end of the world (Revelation 13:11-17; 16:13; 19:20; 20:10). The Bible reveals several ways to identify false prophets:
- They teach sexual immorality and permissiveness: 2 Peter 2:13
- They try to lead people away from obedience to God's Word: Deuteronomy 13:1-5
- They make false claims: Matthew 24:23-24
- They deceive people with miraculous signs: Matthew 24:11, 24
- They do not prophecy according to the proportion of faith (in right relation to God's Word): Romans 12:6
- False prophets do not have the fruit of the Holy Spirit in their lives: Matthew 7:15-16; Galatians 5:22-23
- What they prophesy does not come to pass: Deuteronomy 18:20-22

The Purposes Of Prophecy

This is clearly explained in Harvestime International Network's article *The Prophetic Word of God*,[14] (2010), presented here to cast light on the topic:

---

[14] Ibid, pp. 3-4.

The Bible reveals three main purposes for God speaking to men through prophecy:

1. **To authenticate God's message.**

Fulfilled prophecy proves that God's message is authentic. In Isaiah 41:21-23 God challenges the gods of the heathen nations to prove their power by foretelling future events. They could not do it because they were false gods:

> 'Let them bring them forth, and shew us what shall happen: let them shew the former things, what they be, that we may consider them, and known the latter end of them; or declare us things for to come' (Isaiah 41:22) (KJV).[15]

2. **To confirm God's messenger.**

Prophecy confirms the true messengers of God:

> 'The prophet which prophesieth of peace, when the word of the prophet shall come to pass, then shall the prophet be known, that the Lord hath truly sent him' (Jeremiah 28:9).

3. **To instruct believers.**

Believers are to receive instruction from prophecy and take heed (pay attention) to it:

---

[15] In this section all scripture quotation are from the King James Version of the Bible unless stated otherwise.

'We have also a more sure word of prophecy; whereunto ye do well that ye take heed, as unto a light that shineth in a dark place ...' (2 Peter 1:19).

To fully appreciate the complexity of prophecy one needs to realise that it manifests in more than one form. Most of our current understanding of prophecy is that it is about 'foretelling' something, that it involves making declarations about unknown future events as revealed by God. In other words, it is predicting what will happen in the future. The personal prophecies that some of us may have been fortunate enough to have received, usually relate to what life has in store for us in the future. However, there is another aspect of the prophetic, which is 'forthtelling'. This facet of prophecy is not entirely about looking forward to the future but is rather about speaking forth the heart and Word of God, declaring what God has revealed, His purpose or His will. It deals with present circumstances — what is happening here and now in the present time. Forthtelling may also concern the revelation of events which happened in the past and can, in some cases, deal with the future as well.

Chapter Two

The Process of Prophecy

PROPHETIC REVELATION

Prophetic revelations may be received personally in dreams, visions, or words; or via someone serving as the mouthpiece of God, namely a prophet. In all cases though, prophetic revelation is God communicating with His children and contains guidance and insight the Lord desires to give us.

According to the illuminating article *What does it mean to be prophetic?*[16] (2013), by Stephen Hill of Fatherheart Ministries, the following is of relevance:

2 Peter 1:19-21 says:

'...and we have something more sure, the prophetic word, to which you will do well to pay attention as to a lamp shining

---

[16] Online article: *What does it mean to be prophetic?* by Stephen Hill, Taupo, 2013, pp 2-3, 5. URL: http://www.fatherheart.net/site/fatherheart/files/Articles/Article%20-%20The%20Prophetic.pdf. Permission granted.

in a dark place, until the day dawns and the morning star rises in your hearts,

'knowing this first of all, that no prophecy of Scripture comes from someone's own interpretation.

'For no prophecy was ever produced by the will of man, but men spoke from God as they were carried along by the Holy Spirit' (ESV).[17]

A lamp shining in a dark place is the bringing of revelation to the heart that has not got that revelation. Prophetic revelation is like the dawning of a new day. Personally speaking, when I first heard the prophetic revelation of the love of the Father and that His love could be imparted and that I could live experientially as a son, it was as if a new dawn broke in my heart. It took prophetic preaching to do this – to shine a lamp of revelation into the hidden recesses of my heart.

John 1 – 'John the Baptist came to bear witness to the light, but he was not the light'.

John 5:35 – 'He was a burning and shining lamp, and you were willing to rejoice for a while in his light'.

The prophetic is not the dawn itself, but it is a lamp which shines in the darkness (lack of revelation) until the day dawns. The day dawns when God is fully revealed within the heart of His people

---

[17] The English Standard Version of the Bible is used for scripture quotes in this section unless otherwise indicated.

for who He really is. When the day dawns there is no longer any need for a lamp. When we arrive at the destination there is no longer any need for a sign pointing to it.

[...]

We see an example of Jesus making a prophetic declaration to the woman at the well in John 4:21, 23. He declares to her:

> '...Woman, believe me, the hour is coming when neither on this mountain nor in Jerusalem will you worship the Father...
> 'But the hour is coming, and is now here, when the true worshippers will worship the Father in spirit and in truth, for the Father is seeking such people to worship Him'.

In this statement, He declares the cessation of the old and ushers in the new.

The great prophetic question that God put to some of the prophets in the Old Testament was, "What do you see?" Prophetic ministry is really the answer to that question. Prophetic ministry is really telling what it is seeing. It is prophetic because those who hear it are not seeing what the prophet sees.

The Heart Of God

We need to understand that we were created for the purposes that God intends for us. Each one of us is made by God for a mission to be fulfilled here on earth. We were born to serve God and to represent God's will — our destiny lies with God. When Carol and I first met, we had a gut feeling that there was more to our lives than meets the eye. We understood that we were called by God for a purpose: to make an impact on young people. Our relationship was based on that understanding. We realised that our ministry is our service to the Church and the body of Christ, to those who believe in the Lord Jesus Christ. We also acknowledge that our mission is designed to make an impact on people who do not have a relationship with God. That is what we believe we were called to do. We are placed on the earth to reflect the heart of God in every area of our lives. God is a God of love and we have to display that love to everyone we meet.

To believe and share in the prophetic is a natural extension of our faith since it manifests the passion and emotion of the heart of God, which we know to be our guiding force. According to the article by Stephen Hill of Fatherheart Ministries, *What does it mean to be prophetic?*[18] (2013):

> The prophetic is not only a channel for the words of God, but it manifests the accompanying emotion of the Father in speaking to His children. It is not enough to speak the Word of God — it must be said how God would say it. To be prophetic is to bring the Word of God with His emotion.
>
> I have come across some quotations from theologians which I have found to be very helpful. These quotes have real spiritual life and insight within them and provide a lot of food for thought.

---

[18] Ibid, pp. 6-7, 9, 11.

The Jewish rabbi, Abraham Joshua Heschel (in a book called *The Prophets*),[19] says that the prophetic word is 'a blast from heaven'. He uses an expression - the 'pathos' of God. The word 'pathos' carries the meaning of 'anguished longing'. Heschel writes:

> "The task of the prophet is to convey the Word of God. Yet the word is aglow with the pathos. One cannot understand the word without sensing the pathos. And one could not impassion others and remain unstirred. The prophet should not be regarded as an ambassador who must be dispassionate, in order to be effective."

What he is saying here is that the prophetic word is only effective if the person who gives it has a sense of the emotion that is in God's heart. This is the place where prophetic speaking is uttered from.

Prophetic ministry comes from a place that is connected and exposed to the heart of the Father. Another theologian, Gerhard Von Rad, says that the prophet "has taken a deeper plunge into the reality of God". It is from that 'deeper reality' that the prophetic word comes in order to bring the people into God's heart.

The Father is revealed by the son (sic) who is in His bosom. Living in intimacy, close to the heart of the Father is the place from which He is prophetically revealed.

[...]

---

[19] New York: Harper & Row, 1962. ISBN 0-06-093699-1

The prophetic doesn't teach – it shifts the spiritual atmosphere. The prophetic doesn't have to be fully understood to be effective.

[...]

In the Scriptures you find that prophetic speaking comes out of wilderness. Many of the Old Testament prophets (Moses) came from the wilderness, John the Baptist came from the wilderness. Jesus came into His ministry from the wilderness, as did Paul. Why is this? I believe it is because the prophetic must come from a place where there has been a significant break from what has gone before. Because the prophetic is foundational (Ephesians 2:20), there must be enough distance from the past to make a fresh start. The prophetic, in that sense, brings a rupture in continuity. The wilderness is a place where 'clothing' turns to rags, and where the usual comforts cease. In other words, the things that give identity and comfort are not easy to come by. They must be supplied by God. The desert is a place where cultural noise is silenced and cultural trappings have been stripped bare.

Fulfilling And Restoring God's Plan

According to the article *What does it mean to be prophetic?*[20] (2013), by Stephen Hill, Fatherheart Ministries:

Prophetic ministry must highlight where something has gone

---

[20] Ibid, p. 12.

wrong and has gone astray from what God really wanted. To that extent, it is negative. It critiques the religious status quo. The key thing is that genuine prophetic ministry does not leave people with the negative but it also energises a positive returning to things the way God wants them to be.

In this context, I feel it wise to add:

> 'Love the Lord your God with all your heart and with all your soul and with all your mind and with all your strength' (Mark 12:30) (NKJV).[21]

> 'Remember the former things of old; for I am God, and there is no other; I am God, and there is none like Me,
> 'declaring the end from the beginning and from ancient times things that are not yet done, saying, "My counsel shall stand, and I will accomplish all my purpose," ...
> 'I have spoken, and I will bring it to pass; I have purposed, and I will do it' (Isaiah 46:9-11) (ESV).[22]

> 'And so we have the prophetic word confirmed, which you do well to heed as a light that shines in a dark place, until the day dawns and the morning star rises in your hearts;
> 'knowing this first, that no prophecy of Scripture is of any private interpretation,
> 'for prophecy never came by the will of man, but holy

---

[21] The New King James Version of the Bible.
[22] The English Standard Version of the Bible.

men of God spoke as they were moved by the Holy Spirit. (2 Peter 1:19-21) (NKJV).[23]

The online Bible Study Guides, in their article *Lesson 3: The Major Prophets and You*,[24] *(2010-2016)*, comment:

> The prophecies of the Bible, though many seem strange to the modern reader, are not the writings of mad men or self-proclaimed futurists. Bible prophecy was directly inspired by God. The prophecies are not speculation; the all-powerful Creator God is well able to make world events work out to exactly fulfil His plan. Thankfully, that plan was created with the eternal benefit of every person in mind. (1 Timothy 2:4; 2 Peter 3:9).

ISAIAH, A MAJOR PROPHET

A look at the background of one of the major Old Testament prophets, Isaiah, provides useful information about the process of prophecy and how through time and even today, there are those who seek to deny the divine inspiration for prophecy.

---

[23] The New King James Version of the Bible.
[24] Online article: *Lesson 3: The Major Prophets and You*, from Series 3 - *The Great Teachings of the Bible and What They Mean for You: Exploring the Bible*, Section: *What is Prophecy? - Why should we listen to Bible prophecies?* (2010-2016).
URL: http://www.freebiblestudyguides.org/bible-teachings/exploring-bible-the-major-prophets-and-you.htm.

The United Church of God's 'Beyond Today' online Bible Commentary publication: *Introduction to Isaiah (Isaiah 1)*,[25] informs us:

> The prophet Isaiah was contemporary with Hosea. They delivered their prophecies during the reigns of the same four kings of Judah (1:1; Hosea 1:1). Hosea also mentions a king of Israel during Uzziah's reign, perhaps because the primary focus of Hosea is the people of the northern kingdom. Isaiah's message is directed toward Judah and Jerusalem, and those nations that interact with them. Yet sometimes, it should be noted, Jerusalem is a reference to all 12 tribes of Israel, as they were at one time united under it. In any case, although the message was relevant for the people of Isaiah's day, it was also written as a prophecy for the *end-time* nation of Judah, Israel and the other nations of the world.
>
> Isaiah's actual calling appears to be recorded in chapter 6, and occurs in the final year of Uzziah's reign. The first five chapters serve as a long introduction to the book. The name 'Isaiah' means 'The Eternal Saves' or 'The Eternal Helps', and the deliverance of Judah and Israel, as well as the gentile nations, is a central theme of the book. Isaiah is called the messianic prophet for an obvious reason — his many wonderful prophecies of the coming Deliverer, the Messiah, and the Messiah's coming reign over all nations. That Messiah would, as all professing Christians

---

[25] Extracted in full from United Church of God's 'Beyond Today' Bible Commentary online publication: *Introduction to Isaiah (Isaiah 1)*, March 12. Permission Granted. URL: http://bible.ucg.org/bible-commentary/Isaiah/Sins-of-Israel-and-Judah-like-scarlet/.

understand, be revealed as Jesus Christ. Speaking of Jesus, John 12:41 says that Isaiah 'saw His glory and spoke of Him'. (Isaiah is quoted or referred to 85 times in the New Testament — from 61 separate passages.)

Isaiah is referred to 13 times as the son of Amoz, which may suggest that his father was a man of some prominence. According to Jewish rabbinic tradition in the Babylonian Talmud, this Amoz was a brother of Judah's King Amaziah. If so, this would make Isaiah first cousin to King Uzziah, and a grandson of King Joash — and thus a man of the palace, being of royal blood. Growing up in such an environment, he would have been familiar with international relations and other affairs of state. According to the Babylonian and Jerusalem Talmud, Isaiah was martyred when King Manasseh, apostate son of Hezekiah, had him fastened between two planks and 'sawn asunder' (to which Hebrews 11:37 appears to refer).

'Critical' scholarship — that based in the view that the Bible is not the inspired Word of God nor written when it claims to be — has denied Isaiah's authorship of chapters 40-66. Instead, it attributes this section to a later unknown author it calls 'Deutero-Isaiah', i.e., 'Second Isaiah' though not actually named Isaiah. Others have argued for a third author (Trito-Isaiah) for chapters 55-66. The New Testament, however, quotes from all three sections of the book, attributing each quote to the one biblical prophet Isaiah himself (compare Isaiah 1:9 and Romans 9:29; Isaiah 53:1 and Romans 10:16; Isaiah 65:1 and Romans 10:20).

Why do critics try to post-date Isaiah? *Mainly because Isaiah accurately prophesied future events.* (For example, Isaiah names the Persian ruler Cyrus 200 years before he came to power, Isaiah 44:28; 45:1.) The critics, you see, have a choice: they must either admit that an overseeing supernatural power and intelligence inspired these prophecies or find some other way to explain them. They have gone with the latter solution — redating the prophecies, moving the date of composition forward a few centuries so that the prophecies appear to have been written after all of the prophesied events had already occurred. This has been true of 'higher criticism' for most prophetic books.

The online Bible Study Guides, in their article *Lesson 3: The Major Prophets and You*,[26] add the following commentary:

> Dr Gleason L. Archer examines the theories about multiple authors of the book of Isaiah in two chapters in his book *A Survey of Old Testament Introduction* (1964).[27] He concludes:
>
>> In view of all the foregoing evidence, it may fairly be said that it requires a far greater exercise of credulity to believe that Isaiah 40-66 was not written by the historical eighth-century Isaiah than to believe that it was. Judging from internal evidence alone, even apart from the authority of the New Testament authors, a fair handling of the evidence can only lead to the conclusion that the same author was responsible for both sections and that no part of it was composed as late as the exile.

---

[26] Ibid.
[27] *A Survey of Old Testament Introduction*, Gleason L. Archer. Chicago, Moody Press, 1964. Updated edition: *A Survey of Old Testament Introduction*. Chicago: Moody Press, 1994. ISBN 0-8024-8200-7.

The experience of prophecy that Carol and I have had impacted us in a way very similar to what Isaiah experienced. In the Scripture we find that Isaiah's life changed after his vision of God; as did our lives. While Isaiah may have understood and related to the God of Israel in times past, his view of God and his future were utterly transformed in the year that king Uzziah died. Isaiah realised his own appalling inadequacy and his need to rely on God for everything after he caught a glimpse of God's vastness and holiness.

We have come to realise that we cannot accomplish anything until we have had an encounter with God to clarify our purpose and to provide guidance. Carol and I relate to Isaiah in that we also had to accept that we cannot understand and walk the prophetic path without totally depending on God. While it is worthwhile to consider all the different hands-on opportunities that Christians have to serve Christ and His Church, our service began with honest, open-hearted prayer and personal, one-on-one time with God in His word. Carol and I came to the conclusion that the more we invest in our relationship with God, the more we understand how much we need guidance in our prophetic journey with Him.

Chapter Three

Our Journey and Calling Begin

HIGH SCHOOL YEARS: 1981 TO 1985

In 1981, at the age of fourteen, I began my secondary education at Portland High School in Mitchells Plain, located about 32 km from the city of Cape Town. One night during that year, I had a dream that I was standing on a platform in a crowded auditorium, speaking to thousands of people who were listening attentively. I did not know what it meant as I was young and had started my walk with God only two years prior to having the dream. I spoke to my youth leader at the church and he told me that he believed God was calling me. He encouraged me to read the Old Testament story of Samuel who heard a voice while he was asleep and thought it was Eli calling him (1 Samuel 3).

It was also during this time that I became more and more entangled in politics and was actively part of the 1981 South Africa political unrest in Cape Town. At Portland High School I was a member of the drama club, the leader of the Society for Christian Students (SCS), a student leader (prefect), chairman of COSAS and of the debate team. I would influence the students to oppose the education curriculum imposed on us by the 'white' authorities, and fight against racial oppression.

In 1983, as I was preparing for my year-end exams, I had the same dream about standing in front of thousands of young people, and I saw them crying, calling unto God as they wept. I went to speak to the priest at Christ the Mediator Anglican Church in Portlands, Mitchells Plain. He encouraged me, saying that he believed it was God calling me to the priesthood, and that I should consider becoming an Anglican priest. He also mentioned the story of Samuel that my youth leader had referred to earlier.

In the meantime, I was doing every form of service one could in the church I attended to show my commitment and dedication to God. It was during this time that the priest called me to a special meeting during which the church board had made a recommendation for me to go to the Theological Seminary once I finished school at the end of 1985. The church would help me pay all expenses; all I had to do was sign the paperwork. I left the meeting without signing but very excited and confused at the same time. The dreams I had and now this offer ...? What was God saying? Was this the beginning of what I knew then as the calling of God? In all the confusion one wonders why the Christian path should be so complicated: decisions, decisions, decisions. I shared my experience with my family, and they were not surprised about matters as my mother was always encouraging us to do something significant with our lives. I remember how, when I was a young boy, she would always tell us not to live our lives for ourselves but for others.

In 1985, I was in my final school year and preparing for my future. I was still heavily involved in politics and I wrote a play, *Teachers*

– *Leave the Kids Alone*, which depicted the conflict between whites and blacks in South Africa. The play, including its main musical number, became so well-known that we got invited to perform it on various platforms and at political rallies. It was only during the second half of the year that I became more aware that the social and political agenda in which I was involved, was not going to provide me with a life-long career. I ended up attending a South African Defence Force (SADF) workshop, organised by the school. As a result of this, the students started to see me as a traitor to the cause and a back-stabber, and I had to endure tremendous attack for my decision to consider this career option.

I was also spoken to about this matter by members of the church and Father Karl, our priest at Christ the Mediator Anglican Church in Portlands, who expressed his extreme disappointment in me for not pursuing my calling to the priesthood. The next four months proved to be very stressful as I struggled to prepare for the final examinations of my school career, while working as a casual-employee in a supermarket, and being involved in the SCS. I knew somehow that there was a higher power at play and that it was the power of God.

My parents divorced in 1985; it was a difficult year. The impact it had on me as a teenager was significant and it affected me deeply. I never thought being part of a broken home could be so painful and being so young, I did not understand how much emotional turmoil this environment created for me. The closest I had come to knowing anything about divorce was through the media and television shows. I knew some friends at my school whose parents were divorcing but never thought that I would be joining their ranks.

I believe every teenager and every family are unique and so too, are the reasons for and dynamics of every divorce. It was, therefore, very difficult for me to predict or prescribe how any of my teenage friends would respond to their parents divorcing. I did not understand what they were going through until I encountered it myself and found it to be a terrible experience.

I felt as if we, their children, were the cause of the situation, that our demands as children were the reason for our dad's behaviour. Our mom had to juggle her time and life between work, caring for us seven children and spending time with dad. We did feel guilty to an extent when our parents divorced.

Discovering My Purpose: 1986 To 1990

In January 1986, I started work as a quality controller for R.J. Southey, a sandblasting company in Killarney, Milnerton, Cape Town. Our company's contract had us working at the Koeberg Nuclear Power Station and we used to travel the 30 km north to Koeberg at 5 am every weekday. My manager was a Mr Daniels, who was also our neighbour in Mitchells Plain. I worked in this position for about two months before I was called up to join the South African Navy (SA Navy) in April 1986.

I left home for Saldanha Naval Base in the Western Cape in May 1986, and completed my basic training in September 1986, after which I was transferred to Simon's Town Naval Base as a rookie chef, still serving my apprenticeship and learning from other qualified chefs.

Another significant change I made in 1986 was leaving the Anglican Church to join the Apostolic Faith Mission (AFM), attending their Pentecostal Church in Rocklands, Mitchells Plain.

Carol and I were involved in the youth group at Rocklands AFM Church. The youth of the larger Mitchells Plain church community were divided into the four regions of Westridge, Portlands, Rocklands and Lentegeur. Carol and I were members of the Westridge region's youth group. Westridge was very active in outreach programmes, all-night prayer meetings, youth camps, Bible studies and youth services. I was the 'preacher' or 'evangelist' of the Westridge youth group, and Carol became their secretary.

I recall that most of our time between 1985 and 1993 was spent doing outreach work amongst communities in our region. We would spend almost every Saturday morning conducting open-air youth services with a band providing the music, and I would preach the Gospel while other youth would hand out tracts — our reading material on how to be saved from the consequences of your sins. Most Saturday evenings would be spent attending Gospel concerts and braai (barbecue) events. We would frequently visit other youth groups and share our faith together.

In 1987, I had the same dream again that I had had when I was fourteen and sixteen years old, with me standing in front of thousands of young people and preaching. I went to speak to the pastor of the Rocklands AFM Church and his words to me were, "It is clear that God has a calling on your life but you should go work and not think of full-time ministry as you are still very young." That was not the answer I wanted to hear. I thought he was going to tell me to quit my Navy job and go into full-time ministry.

I continued developing my career as a chef in the SA Navy and in July 1987, went off to the Naval Catering School at Simonsberg to complete my training as a chef. I put my skills to good use and would do catering on our youth camps, cooking for up to two hundred young people at any one time.

In 1988, I felt a deep sense of calling and enrolled at the Sarepta Bible College in Kuils River, in the Western Cape province (25 km east of Cape Town), as a part-time student whilst still serving as a chef in the SA Navy. I was unaware that this would be the start of me following the recurring dream I had been having since a young age. My arrangement of working as a chef during the day and travelling to Bible College at night to study theology, did not work very well. My position as a chef on serving ships in the Navy required that I be away from home for long periods of time. At the same time, we were obliged to attend the Bible College in person at least three nights a week, and on a fourth evening we had an extra session with our lecturers to receive mentoring and discuss our assignments which we had to keep up to date. At this college we completed written exams as for any other education institution.

In 1989, as the final Bible College exams were approaching, I went away on a thirty-day work assignment and knew I was going to miss out on my course finals due to circumstances beyond my control. When I returned from my naval duty, I was informed by my lecturer that I would not be able to complete my studies that year, and that I would not be allowed a special opportunity for a catch-up exam in the near future. I was to do the two years all over again. I was devastated. I did not understand this turn of events even though I felt a calling, a conviction that God was ultimately in control of the time schedule of my life.

That did not mean that the calling by God was no longer there only that the timing was a challenge for me. David was sixteen years old when he was anointed to be king of Israel. He continued to look after his father's sheep until God's timing was perfect for him to reign. Divine calling is not only a calling to preach, it is about being set apart for a specific purpose and assignment. We are all called by God for a purpose. It is when we choose to follow that purpose that our lives acquire meaning.

The easiest way to discover the purpose of an invention is to ask the invention's creator what it is. The same applies for our purpose in life. We need to ask our creator about our purpose. I learned early on in life that my purpose and identity begin with the relationship I have with Jesus Christ. I had to accept Him as the source of my purpose in life and my reason for living, by answering His divine calling.

I also found out that long before my parents thought of having me, I was on the mind of God. Another lesson I learnt at an early age was that my life's purpose fits into a bigger purpose God has for the world and eternity. Together with other individuals we form part of God's divine plan and this gives our lives meaning.

My teenage years were filled with both happiness and sadness, and I had to make a choice to either give in to the negatives or pursue the dream that I was passionate about, namely people and their salvation. I chose the latter, and it was a conscious decision. Without God, life would not make sense to me.

Carol and I were friends in the youth community for quite a while, socialising together around other youth members and friends, and not yet interested in each other on any other level. We started dating after Christmas 1989. During the first week of February 1990, Carol and I were at a prayer meeting when one of the ladies of the church, Sister Fredericks said, "I am part of a ladies prayer and intercessory group, and there is a sister in the group called Jackie

Dicks, and she had a dream about you." Not knowing what this meant, we agreed to meet with this lady. We ended up at her home about three days later, and found that she was familiar to me. My twin brother, Abraham, was dating her daughter, and she had once come to fetch her daughter at our home. Standing there in front of her, I was rather fearful since I had come to know her as a prophet of God and knew that she was never wrong in every word received from God that she gave to people.

We shared a little fellowship and then she started praying for us. During her prayers she gave us this revelation from God: "God is doing something in your lives. He says that you are called for greatness and you should wait on Him. You are going to wear many hats in your life." (*Prophecy One.*) We were amazed. We were young and did not understand what prophecy was and how it worked. We left her house excited that we had had an encounter with God.

I remember another occasion, later that same year, when she called me and prophesied over my life, saying, "God is showing me that you have things in your life that He is not happy with and you need to break free, break free — and let God do a good thing for you." (*Prophecy Two.*) I wanted more of this as a young man.

I started to realise that having a prophet speaking about our lives was as if it God himself was speaking, and it was awesome. Carol and I started showing an interest in each other, showing an inclination to be more than just church youth members socialising together. We became more and more aware of something unique happening in our lives and we wanted to explore the opportunity. We were constantly aware of the process of God working in our lives and the journey of faith we were on.

In May 1990, I left the SA Navy and joined the South African Police Force (SAPF) in July 1990. Carol and I started seeing each other more frequently. Our time together consisted of praying and Bible study. We continued to attend youth meetings, midweek prayer meetings at church, and Sunday church services. In this early stage of our friendship, Carol's parents were very excited to see their daughter in a relationship with a 'godly man', as they always put it. They had a very good relationship with me at that time. We always spoke about the goodness of Jesus whenever we were together at their home.

In May 1990, Sister Jackie contacted me and asked that we pray together at her home as she had had a dream about me. I decided to take Carol along and we met with her. Sister Jackie said, "I had a dream and I saw you standing in front of a man in a uniform. I see an aeroplane and you hand him a paper. I cannot see what is written on the paper but it is stamped with some sort of government stamp. I also see Carol there as you turn around and she is waving at you. Read Psalm 51." (*Prophecy Three.*)

We continued to pray together and it was awesome. We felt the presence of the Lord as we spoke in tongues for over an hour. At the end of 1990, I bought my first house as a young man.

Our Relationship Is Tested: 1991

The relationship between Carol and me started to develop into more than friendship. We shared a strong feeling of wanting to do God's will. I approached Carol's dad to ask him if we could start our courtship. He was so excited about it, but her mother was not as happy. Carol and I became engaged in August 1991. Then things started to turn bad and go wrong for our relationship in respect of her family's feelings towards me. It was like Satan was let loose over us. Carol and I continued to do outreach ventures as a couple and with the Westridge youth. We did prison visits, hospital visits and the work of evangelism. Carol played the guitar and sang to the prisoners, and to the sick and elderly in retirement villages.

One evening I went to pick Carol up at her mother's house for a prayer meeting. I stood there dressed in a tidy, formal church outfit with a Bible in my hand. To my dismay, her mother did not gladly welcome me. I was shocked. I was not aware at the time that this was part of the attack by Satan, the enemy, who was standing in the way of God's plan for our lives. I was mistreated by her brother and mother and falsely accused by her sister.

Back then in our community, men in service with the police or defence force — men in uniform in general — were considered to have little character. They were stigmatised as being men who would use their uniform, the authority and influence it represented, to attract women for relationships and marriage. This was probably how Carol's family perceived me. I tried to defend myself but it was in vain, and I felt humiliated. The only thing going through my mind was: what have I done to deserve this? I went home and locked myself in my room. Don't get me wrong; when I look back on the incident now, I understand that every mother would protect her daughter at all cost. This is what Carol's mother, brothers and sisters were simply trying to do. Carol and I did not understand it then, and we embraced the rough road we had to endure to accomplish what God had in store for us.

Matters soon became worst for us. Our families grew apart and we had to consider whether to end our relationship or disregard the wishes of her family and continue seeing each other behind their backs. We also had to decide if we were going to involve any of her family in the plans for our future. Carol's family were very close-knit and it was hard for her to see them not accepting me. There were days when the situation became almost unbearable, but we had to stay focussed on what God had said to us through prophecy. In our culture, once a couple are engaged they start to work on the preparations for their wedding with the help of the parents of both their families. In our case, this did not happen due to Carol's parents not granting their blessing for us to get married. On three occasions I asked her parents' permission to marry their daughter, and it was denied three times.

Carol's parents said they were disappointed in me because of all the negative rumours they had heard about me. They felt that I would become like my father whom my mother had divorced and who had been living in adultery. Well, this was a stigma that I had been carrying for a while because many people said the same thing about me, namely that I would be the man my father was. What a load to carry when people label you in this way; it only truly matters how God sees you. I was not welcome at Carol's parents' home, and Carol eventually had to make a decision about whether she would continue to see me, or conform to her parents' wishes and end our relationship. This made me angry at God and the world, because I did not yet understand the process of God's hand at work.

On one occasion, as I was driving home from work and approaching the Mitchells Plain entrance, close to Carol's home, I noticed a traffic accident. I saw emergency vehicles and a rescue helicopter at the scene. I drove closer and recognised Carol's dad's car — it was badly damaged in the crash. Immediately, I felt sick and nauseous. The only thing I could do was say a prayer, "Lord, please let them be okay, please save their lives." At this point I rushed to Carol at their home and quickly went inside to see if she was okay. I received a cold shoulder from her brother but I ignored him as my only concern was Carol's well-being. I escorted Carol to the hospital since she was anxious and shaken-up emotionally. At the hospital Carol's mother was being attended to by a nurse in an emergency treatment area. I walked in with Carol, and her mother asked me to leave the room. I knew that I was not welcome, so I left and waited for Carol in the carpark.

When I look back over the course of my life, I realise the extent to which the devil would go to steal, kill or destroy the plan God has for our lives – using those closest to us to derail His plan. From a young age I was devoted to my family and would let nothing come between us. Well, this was a sensitive issue for me, especially with Carol's family not giving our relationship their blessing. Their lack of involvement in our lives as a couple, and my treatment at the hands of her family affected me emotionally. As someone from a broken family, it was challenging for me to try to fit into her family which was so closely bound together, and I was struggling to make sense of it all. On many occasions, Carol's parents would not want her to go to church with me, let alone to any church functions. But I do believe this was just a demonstration of how the devil goes the extra mile to divert you from what God wants.

Many a time while Carol was conducting her devotion and having intimate moments with the Heavenly Father, her parents would interrupt by yelling at her because they had a negative view of this type of worship. Of course, this made us stronger in our faith and our walk with God. It was still confusing as to why Carol's family would not accept me as her future husband. We believed this was just the work of Satan, the enemy since we knew that God had a greater plan for our lives. It became so bad that at one stage we decided to give up on our relationship and not cause any more pain to her family. I prayed daily that God would take control and set His plan in motion.

It was then that Sister Jackie invited Carol and me to her home to share a time of prayer with her. I had mixed emotions about accepting her request as we were on the verge of ending our relationship to please Carol's family. Carol and I decided to give it another go and allow God to take control of our relationship.

It was around December 1991 when we had our scheduled prayer session with Sister Jackie. On arriving at her door, she said, "I had a dream and God showed me that you should write down the date 6 June, I don't know what this means but it must be important if God says it." (*Prophecy Four.*) We continued talking and started praying. During that prayer-time I clearly heard: "My son, I have chosen you for purpose." It was so real. I believed I had an encounter with God and that put my mind at ease.

I continued in my belief that our lives are predestined long before we were conceived, and that God is ultimately in control of our destiny and future.

In his book *The Purpose Driven Life,*[28] (2002), Pastor Rick Warren reaffirms that God created us each for a purpose:

> The church is a body, not a building; an organism, not an organization. We discover our role in life through our

---

[28] *The Purpose-Driven Life: What on earth am I here for?* Richard Warren. Grand Rapids, Zondervan, 2002. Day 17: A Place to Belong. Permission Granted.

relationships with others. For the organs of your body to fulfil their purpose, they must be connected to your body. The same is true for you as a part of Christ's Body. You were created for a specific role, but you will miss this purpose of your life if you're not attached to a living, local church.

The Bible tells us:

> 'In this way we are like the various parts of a human body. Each part gets its meaning from the body as a whole, not the other way around. The body we're talking about is Christ's body of chosen people. Each of us finds our meaning and function as a part of his body. But as a chopped-off finger or cut-off toe we wouldn't amount to much, would we? So since we find ourselves fashioned into all these excellently formed and marvellously functioning parts in Christ's body' (Romans 12:4-5) (MSG).[29]

According to Pastor Rick Warren, as presented in his online article *Molded*[30] *into Godly Character,*[31] (2014):

> God uses his Word, people, and circumstances to mold (*sic*) us. All three are indispensable for character development. God's

---

[29] The Message Bible Version.
[30] The USA English spelling of this word has been preserved in the title and quoted material.
[31] Pastor Rick's Daily Hope website's online article: *Molded into Godly Character*, 21 May 2014. Permission Granted. URL: http://pastorrick.com/devotional/english/molded-into-godly-character_657

Word provides the truth we need to grow, God's people provide the support we need to grow, and circumstances provide the environment to practice Christlikeness.

If you study and apply God's Word, connect regularly with other believers, and learn to trust God in difficult circumstances, I guarantee you will become more like Jesus.

Pastor Rick Warren continues[32]:

Many people assume all that is needed for spiritual growth is Bible study and prayer. But some issues in life will never be changed by Bible study or prayer alone. God uses people. He usually prefers to work through people rather than perform miracles, so that we will depend on each other for fellowship. He wants us to grow together.

In many religions, the people considered to be the most spiritually mature and holy are those who isolate themselves from others in mountaintop monasteries, uninfected by contact with other people.

But this is a gross misunderstanding. Spiritual maturity is not a solitary, individual pursuit!

You cannot grow to Christlikeness in isolation. You must be around other people and interact with them. You need to be a part of a church and community.

Why? Because true spiritual maturity is all about learning to love like Jesus, and you can't practice being like Jesus without being in relationship with other people.

Remember, it's all about love - loving God and loving others.

---

[32] Ibid.

Bob Deffinbaugh in his article *The Purpose of Prophecy*,[33] (2016), in the Bible.org series: *God's Final Word on the Last Times — A Study on the Book of Revelation*, comments:

> We have every reason to expect prophecy to be literally fulfilled, but we have little basis for supposing that we, at this point in time, can suggest precisely and dogmatically just how this will take place. Let us be suspicious of every neatly packed prophetic scheme, for why should we think we are better able to predict the specifics of our Lord's second coming when the prophets of old were unable to outline the events of the first?

In February 1992, Carol and I had an encounter with God. We were friends with a couple, Alan Wilcox and his wife, who were called to service in the realm of demonic deliverance. Alan and I had worked together at the Simon's Town Naval Base, ministering and evangelising to sailors and staff, telling them about Jesus. We still kept in contact even after I left the Navy, and we would visit them frequently from 1987 onward — and even more so after Carol and I started dating in early 1990. Carol and I would spend time praying with the Wilcox couple. They invited us to participate in a deliverance session at their home to help them pray for a young girl who was demon-possessed.

Although we did not understand what this entailed, we knew we wanted to be part of what God required of us as a couple. Alan

---

[33] Section 3 of the online article: *The Purpose of Prophecy*, by Bob Deffinbaugh, 2016, from The Bible.org series: *God's Final Word on the Last Times — a Study on the Book of Revelation*. Permission Granted. URL: https://bible.org/seriespage/purpose-prophecy.

Wilcox and his wife were wonderful people who were used by God to do His work. Since this event took place during the Apartheid years, we had to be very careful not to be seen together in public because they were 'white' and we were 'brown' people and were not legally permitted to socialise with one another. We secretly went to their Muizenberg apartment, which was in a very 'white' suburb (only those officially classified as racially white were allowed to live there). There we encountered what we believed was a demonic spirit. As we were praying for the young girl's deliverance, the evil spirit manifested itself and physically threw the girl against the wall and spoke in a husky voice. At the end of the day, God's power prevailed and the girl was released from its grasp and delivered from the evil spirit. That encounter made me realise how important it was to stay focussed on what God wanted to achieve through our lives as a couple.

It was not long after this incident that Carol and I met up with Sister Jackie again, and we spent several visits praying with her, seeking God's guidance for our future. On one occasion she prophesied: "God loves the two of you and he want to use you. I see a river flowing and I see you two standing next to it with a Bible in your hands. God is preparing your journey. Read Jeremiah 1:4–10." (*Prophecy Five.*) We were more than assured that we had a divine purpose in our lives.

By March 1992, issues in our personal lives had not gotten any better. The Westridge youth members and the church were very supportive and the youth leader, Brian Benting, was like a big brother and mentor to me. He was always there for us, to encourage us and imprint the Scriptures and Word of God upon our hearts. Brian was eventually the one chosen to give Carol away on our wedding day, considering that her family did not want to be part of anything in our lives. This, of course, took an emotional toll on Carol as she loved her family dearly.

By this time, Carol's dad was on crutches and his health was deteriorating. He was a diabetic and was losing his eyesight. I was still not welcome to visit Carol at her parents' house, and was still being placed under a lot of pressure by Carol's family to leave her alone and end our relationship. It was clear that our relationship was putting a strain on her family, and they refused to see God's hand over our lives. They would go to extremes to make their frustration known, made efforts to separate the two of us, and interfered in our relationship. This made Carol and me question once again whether we should remain in a relationship or give in to her family's wishes.

Our relationship was under physical, emotional and spiritual attack. We had to seek the face of God more than ever before as the negative factors in our lives became greater than the positive ones. But God will turn our negatives into positives, if we just trust Him. And that is what Carol and I did. We trusted God to give us direction and lead us the way forward. Don't misunderstand me — our families are a blessing, but even 'family' can stand in the way, coming between you and God's purpose. As we spent more time with God the message became clearer and clearer to us: "God is in control and we must remain in His will." Yes, we loved our families but we had to make a decision and we did. To follow Christ we paid the price of having to leave our families and embark on our journey of prophecy without them. It caused much strife between our families but, thank God, over time He has brought love, peace and unity amongst us.

The decision Carol and I made created unease in our church because the pastor of our congregation was aware of the strain between me and the Daniels family. Our pastor was very supportive in prayer and guided us through this process. We went to see Sister Jackie, wanting to spend time with her in prayer as by now she had become our spiritual mother and our prophet. We needed support in prayer.

Chapter Four

Overcoming Challenges

MARRIAGE AND A PROMOTION: 1992

In March 1992, Carol's dad passed away and this was hard on Carol as she was very close to him. His death was a painful experience for both of us, and it created an even greater barrier between her family and me. Almost from the start of my relationship with Carol, her family said that I brought bad luck into their home and would blame me for anything bad that happened to them. Often when Carol's mother and father disagreed on something, they would attribute the cause to our relationship. You can imagine the pressure on us as a young couple. We surrendered our situation to God, wanting Him to work it out for us. During this time we maintained our love for Carol's family and did not harbour any bitterness or hatred, or withhold forgiveness.

A week after the funeral of Carol's father, we went to visit Sister Jackie. She told us: "I had a dream about the two of you. God showed me a shop in Adderley Street, Cape Town, and I see the name 'Mayer' in the dream. You need to go there and God will show when the time is right to do so. You should also know that you will go through a storm before your wedding day. I see angels hovering over the two of you ... just remain strong and stay focussed. Read Isaiah 54. God is saying He will not let any weapon prosper against you as long as you stay faithful." (*Prophecy Six.*) We continued to pray and God blessed our time together.

At this stage, Carol and I decided it was time to start planning our wedding. The day we selected for our marriage was 6 June 1992, but encountered some obstacles with this choice so we tried to set an earlier date and then also a later date, but every time we would revert back to and agree on 6 June. Carol and I recalled that the prophecy received from Sister Jackie some time ago, mentioned 6 June. We found that our congregation's church was not available for a marriage service on our chosen date so we contacted the local Baptist Church. More pieces fell into place when we discovered 6 June was the only available date they had to host our wedding and that, due to his busy schedule, the pastor was not available on any other day. These coincidences served as confirmation to us that we should secure 6 June as our wedding day. I went back to Carol's mother to ask one more time for Carol's hand in marriage but was declined.

The hiring company we identified as the supplier for the reception gear was fully booked for June but, another fortuitous sign, on further investigation found they had a cancellation for 6 June. They could accommodate our requirements and provide everything necessary for the reception. I decided that I was going to do the catering myself, since I was the kitchen manager at the SA Police Academy kitchens in Bishop Lavis, 15 km east of Cape Town's city centre.

With our date set and no positive response from Carol's family, it was clear we had to do this on our own with only God's help.

We believed that God was in control and did not want us to divert from the prophecy that had been spoken. I had my family's support and they all agreed to assist with the wedding arrangements. Carol did not have a wedding dress yet as we were in the early stages of planning the wedding. She spoke about the type of dress she always wanted and even made a drawing of it.

Our wedding arrangements well underway, Carol and I went on an outing to Cape Town in April 1992. We were about to cross the main road, Adderley Street, when our attention was drawn to a storefront signage 'Mayer Bridal Shop'. Then while we were walking, I remembered and now understood the prophecy made by Sister Jackie who in her vision saw the name 'Mayer'. I immediately looked at Carol and we decided to visit the shop. As we entered something profound happened. The owner of the shop, whom we had never met nor seen before, came straight towards us and said, "I was praying last night and guess what? God told me that you were going to come into the store today. He described you in detail. Come, I have just the dress you need, and you do not have to pay for it as I would like you to wear the bridal gown to advertise our company amongst the coloured and black people of your community." We were blown away. The bridal gown was an exact copy of the drawing Carol had made of her 'dream' wedding dress — and it also fitted her perfectly. It was like a wish come true. We walked out of the shop in tears, marvelling at how God was bringing prophecy to fulfilment. This event strengthened our faith, with us being so young and not understanding the prophetic realm to the full. We were determined in wanting more of God and learning about His plan for our lives.

In the days ahead we spent longer periods of time in prayer as well as more time with Sister Jackie. These occasions increasingly became a mechanism of escape from the challenges we were facing, all of which were designed to derail our plans and dilute our focus. Carol remained in her mother's house even while her family intensified their disapproval of our wedding. It was during this time that we found refuge in the presence of God, and we spent an increasing amount of time ministering at hospitals and retirement villages to distract us from the issues associated with our impending marriage.

Two weeks before the wedding, we experienced another incident which we felt was God preparing us for what was about to happen. On this occasion, Carol and I were fasting and praying when, during one of our prayer sessions, we clearly experienced God speaking to us. It was as if the room was filled with heaviness and this prompted us to delve deeper into the Spirit of God. Sister Jackie called us a while later and said, "Everything looks good and God is in control, but it is not going to be smooth sailing as the enemy is not happy with what God is doing in your lives." (*Prophecy Seven.*) We started to spend more time praying and trusting God.

By 5 June 1992, all the plans for our wedding had fallen into place. That morning I was alone at home and on leave from my job. I was finishing my quiet time and I could sense that something was not sitting right because I had this unsettling feeling in my spirit. I was excited because it was the day before our wedding and also optimistic about finding out what God was going do for us in our marriage.

My thoughts were interrupted by a telephone call from Pastor A. Jacobs, asking me to come to the church as the hiring company (Mukhtar Hiring Services) had arrived at the church to deliver the reception supplies, and I needed to be there to pay for the items. I was so excited, and jumped in my car to drive to the closest ATM to withdraw the funds. As I was standing in front of the ATM I felt a heaviness descending on me. I tried to withdraw the amount needed but all I got was a message on the screen: "No funds available 0.000". I repeated the process several times to no avail. I found the situation to be impossible because that day was our payday when our salaries are transferred to our accounts by our employer. Walking away from the ATM I was downhearted and devastated because the hiring company would not leave the items at the venue unless they were paid. I immediately drove back home, shut the door, fell on my knees and cried out to God. I wept like a small child, quoting Scripture and reminding God of His Word. I was never as heartbroken as I was at that moment — the risk of the wedding not taking place was high.

Eventually, after spending a substantial amount of time praying, I got up and knew I had to rush down to the church, even though I did not know what I was going to do. As I was standing in the bathroom preparing to leave, I heard a soft voice saying, "God is in control." I got into my car quoting the Word of God, and I said, "Lord your word says that whatsoever we ask in your name we will receive. Your word says you will never leave us nor forsake us. Your word says that you will fight the battle for us."

I finally pulled up at the church and noticed the driver, a Muslim man, had already unloaded the supplies for the wedding and was waiting for me to collect the payment I owed. Before I got out of the car, I asked God to put appropriate words in my mouth and to take full control of the situation. I approached the driver and said, "The price has been paid," meaning that Jesus has paid the price already. The man looked at me very strangely, turned around and set off to call his office to enquire whether the payment had been received. While he was gone, I continued praying in my heart and mind, trusting God to provide a solution. The delivery man returned from the church's office and said, "I am sorry, sir, no one has made a payment." I repeated the same words I had used earlier, more than three times, and could see the man was becoming frustrated with me. Eventually, the driver made a suggestion, saying, "I will leave the items for the wedding reception and not take them back, but if we do not receive the money by 3 pm this afternoon, I will come back and pick up all of it." It was as if God was buying me some time.

The driver left and I got into my car. Driving home, I continued talking to God. Once at home, I fell on my knees and wept before God. I must have become so tired praying and crying that I did not keep track of the time. On her way home from work, Carol dropped by my house and she found me in a sad state. We decided that we would continue to trust God because we both believed that God would not bring us this far to leave us in the lurch.

Then around 1.30 pm, we heard a knock on the front door. At first I was hesitant to open the door but finally convinced myself to do it. My best man was standing on my doorstep; he had decided to pay us a visit. Trevor, who was not a Christian, worked with me at the Police College. He asked me what was wrong because he could see that I was crying. I shared with him what had happened and he replied, "Come with me, I want to show you something." We left my house and drove to the shopping mall where I remained in the car still praying and trusting God, while he went inside. Not long after that Trevor came back to the car, handed me a white envelope and said, "Two months ago you loaned me money and you never asked for it to be repaid. This morning I was at home and my mother told me to give you and Carol a wedding gift. I remembered the money

I owed you and here it is." I could not believe it. When I looked in the envelope it was the exact amount that I needed to cover all the outstanding wedding expenses. I was completely stunned by God's act of provision.

The hiring company was only 30 minutes away from where we were, and I knew I had to rush over to make the payment. On my way there I was hurrying and unintentionally exceeding the speed limit. A traffic officer soon noticed my speeding car and pulled me over. As I rolled down the window to address him, he looked at me and removed his helmet. I found to my astonishment that he was one of my best high-school friends. I was stunned and I tried to explain to him why I was rushing and where I was going. To my delight, he offered to escort me to Mukhtar Hiring Services, so with loud sirens and blinking lights he allowed me free passage without any traffic interference. I considered that to be a miracle. As we pulled up at the hiring company's premises, I noticed the driver I had met earlier getting into his truck. I immediately jumped out of my car and stopped him. He said, "You are a lucky man because I was about to go and pick up your wedding reception supplies." I knew it was not luck but rather God performing a miracle for me and looking out for my best interest. I also knew it was prophecy coming to fulfilment.

I drove back to my house, went down on my knees and could not stop praying, giving thanks to God. Later, I met up with Trevor and shared my testimony with him. Carol and I proceeded with our wedding preparations with Carol adding the finishing touches to the arrangements. We spent the rest of the day with my family, poring over the finer details. The day of our wedding arrived and God really came through for us. God smiled on us and we had a blessed day, a beautiful day as God had promised. The sad part of our 'biggest' day was that Carol's entire family was absent from the wedding, although her brother, Craig, secretly attended.

On 6 June 1992, our wedding day, Carol was happy to be a bride, but felt sad because her mother and siblings were not there to share her special day, especially since she was the baby in the family, the youngest of eight children. I wanted to make it right, and decided to take her back to her mother's house after our wedding reception, for her to say her goodbyes to her parents before we went to my house in Strandfontein. We set out after the reception and as we approached her parents' house, I started to get butterflies in my stomach. Carol went inside to see her family while I waited in the car. She was gone for about 30 minutes and then we left to start our lives as a couple.

We did not have time for a honeymoon as we both had to be back at work a week later. Carol and I always spoke about not having children until two years into our marriage. We wanted to allow God to work in us and use us for His glory. We wanted to establish ourselves in this path and in our marriage before starting a family. Our intention was to give our child everything we thought was required to raise a child well, including our full attention. We spent plenty of time praying about this and made a commitment to God that we would like to enter ministry fulltime once we reach the age of fifty. Carol and I always had a passion for missions and ministry and having a child would be an extra blessing.

Later that month, Sister Jackie called and asked us to spend time in prayer with her because she had dreamt about us. When we finally met up for prayer, she shared her dream with us. She said, "I saw the two of you standing next to a river, there are lots of people and you two are feeding them. I saw you moving from your house very soon, you will know when it's time. Just know that is all in God's plan for your lives. Carol will not understand this now, but just allow God to do the work. Write down the date 2 November, this is what I see God showing me. I don't know what it means. Continue to trust God." (*Prophecy Eight.*) We stayed for coffee and then left.

In the first week of September 1992, I was offered a promotion in the Police Force — an opportunity to become the manager of their kitchens in Paarl, a rural town which was located 150 km from Cape Town, in the Western Cape. It would mean a move for us from Strandfontein and relocation away from our families. We did not know anyone in Paarl. I was not thrilled or excited about it as we had only recently married, had barely started settling into life as a married couple, and I was less than three years into paying my mortgage. I knew I had to seek God's guidance during this type of transition, realising that any change in my life and circumstances was bound to be significant in some way in God's purpose for us.

My commanding officer wanted a response as to my acceptance or not of the new appointment, by end of October 1992. I went home on the day the promotion was offered to me and spoke to Carol about it. She was not ready for this type of move, and said that she had not heard any confirmation from God about it, nor was she willing to make any hasty decision. I was a bit taken aback by her reply, but I left it in God's hands to show us what to do and where to go next. That evening we made it a priority to fast and pray about this decision and we asked God for a sign to indicate the choice he wanted us to make.

Around the middle of October 1992, while we were coming home from church one Sunday evening, we learned that our neighbours' house had been burgled. This had happened even though their house was fortified with security bars on the windows and doors. Our house, on the other hand, had no metal burglar bars or security system installed; consequently, it would have been easier for a burglar to enter our house than theirs. When we arrived home, all I could think of was that maybe this was a sign for us to move out and leave the area. I spoke to Carol that evening and tried again to convince her to agree to a move away from the city. The reply was still, "No, and not until God says so." Carol was so focussed on wanting to be sure of making the right decision.

A week later, around the second last Sunday of the month, we came back from church in the evening and found the Police at our neighbours' house again. We did not make much of it but it was rather a curious situation. Later we found out that their home had been burgled for a second time. Our neighbours were very frustrated about this and decided they were going to move out of the area. At bedtime, I tried again to convince Carol to consider moving. Carol believed that God would not use misfortune, such as our neighbours had experienced, as a sign to convince us to move. I left the discussion at that. The following day, I accepted the offer of promotion and was willing to travel the 150 km round trip to work, daily.

On 30 October 1992, we celebrated Carol's birthday. The following day we were out shopping and when we returned home we received news that two more houses in the same street as ours had been burgled. We did not make much of it as we were content with what God was doing in our lives, not realising that these crimes were playing a role in the confirmation we were seeking from God with regard to making the correct choice about whether or not to relocate.

One evening in early November 1992, while we were having dinner, out of nowhere Carol said, "I want to move and live where it is safer to raise a child." We were unaware that the date was 2 November because we were so busy and preoccupied that day. We only realised it was the significant date Sister Jackie had mentioned when we were having our devotion at bedtime and happened to look at the calendar. It dawned on us that there was a greater power at play in our lives. We just had to allow God to bring His purpose to fulfilment in us. We became more 'hungry' for God in our hearts and His will for us.

By mid-November 1992, I was preparing for my new position in Paarl and we had agreed that I would travel to Paarl daily while Carol would travel (a 50 km round trip) to teach in Cape Town. We also agreed not to have any children until God allowed it to happen.

In December 1992, my manager, Captain Keller, came to see me. He mentioned to me that I qualified for a Police-owned, rental property on the Police Academy premises in Paarl. The rental property was reserved exclusively for Police staff, and the rental was set at only 10% of the tenant's monthly income since it attracted a government subsidy. I would pay around R100.00 (South African Rand) per month for the rental. During this time when Apartheid policies were in effect, I would be the first non-white policeman to occupy a subsidised rental property. I agreed, and we signed all the paperwork. I was to move into the Paarl property in April 1993 and was beyond excited. It became clearer that once again God was working on our behalf. I went home that night and shared the great news with Carol. We saw it as a Christmas gift and could not wait to move.

We spent the entire Christmas holiday period with family, talking about and contemplating our move away from them. It was a very stressful time as our families were very critical and sceptical about this turn of events. Carol's mother would constantly reiterate her disapproval of me. Since I was still not allowed at Carol's family home in Westridge, her mother's house, I would drop Carol off there for a visit while I would go to my family home in Portlands.

Finding A New Home: 1993

On Thursday, 20 February 1993, I was approached by my manager with disappointing news. I was informed that some white police officers had lodged complaints about me being granted a subsidised government house when there were white police officers who were entitled to it and should receive preference over me because I was a brown or 'coloured' police officer. I was devastated because only a week prior, I had listed my Strandfontein house for sale. I was afraid to go home to tell Carol the news and was also extremely upset because I was becoming attached to Paarl.

Since November 1992, I had been travelling daily from Strandfontein to Paarl to work, and I would visit the Paarl Assembly of the Apostolic Faith Mission Church where Pastor L. Maralack was the leader. The Paarl congregation came to know me well because I attended church services there during the week, while on Sundays I attended church services in my home town of Strandfontein.

I did not know how to break the bad news to Carol. A friend of mine, from the Department of Correctional Services, called me at work that day and suggested that I apply for a house at the Drakenstein Prison's residential village. They were leasing staff accommodation to Police and Correctional Service staff at the same price level as I had been offered by the Police Service. This sounded encouraging and I decided to give it a try. I managed to get an appointment with someone at Correctional Services for the following day. As I was driving home that afternoon, I had fellowship with the Holy Spirit. I felt a very real presence with me in the car and this continued for more than an hour. During this time I felt what I believed was the Holy Spirit, and I heard these words: "I am in control - rest in me and see." I was so overwhelmed. Once at home, I shared with Carol what I had encountered that day. Carol was sad but we prayed and decided to trust God.

We contacted Sister Jackie to help us pray. She said, "God is in control and He loves you. I was praying for you yesterday, and God showed me that you are standing in the backyard of a brown house, looking toward the mountain. You should just trust God and see the salvation that He has in store for the two of you." (*Prophecy Nine.*) Maybe I was hoping to hear more than that, considering that she was a prophet and was instrumental in our journey with God. We considered her our spiritual mother and our guardian angel. I knew it came down to simply trusting God and not worrying too much about our dilemma.

The following day, Friday, 21 February 1993, Carol and I went to the Correctional Services property to view the house that they had available for us in the residential village. As we entered the property the houses looked good — big and well maintained, three and four-bedroom houses. We were so excited when we drove among the houses, having no clue which one of them it would be, but we were hoping that it was one of the houses we saw as we entered. The woman who was going to escort us to the property we had been allocated, met with us to drive us there. Our mood suddenly started to change when we noticed that we were driving away from the staff houses. Then we approached an open field and in the middle of the field stood an old, dilapidated, damaged farm house with no windows, and an outhouse toilet situated 20 metres away. It was one of the 19th century homes in that district. We thought the woman was taking a detour past it until she stopped, got out and introduced us to the house intended for us. "It's that farm house," she said.

I took a deep breath, gulped and swallowed, then stared at Carol. We walked towards the house, holding onto each other, and wept. We could not stop crying. The woman looked at us and went to sit in her car. Carol and I held each other and stood there, numb. We said, "God, how can this be happening? We have trusted you with our lives. What have we done to deserve this? Please God, make this go away. Help us." We just stood there for about 15 minutes and finally decided to leave. The woman dropped us off at our vehicle and we left the correctional facility's property. Carol and I were silent, in shock, and could not say a word. At this point you might be having the same thought ... Where is God in this? Maybe you should read further and then you will see the hand of God at work.

We stopped at the side of the road and cried. We prayed and wept for a while as we sat in the car waiting for a word from the Lord. Finally, we drove off and then something amazing happened. I drove for about 10 minutes when I saw the face of Pastor Maralack in my mind's eye, like a photo being paraded in front of me. I stopped the car, looked at Carol, and said, "I just saw Pastor Maralack. I don't know what it means but it must have some importance." Carol just stared at me and did not reply. We continued our journey, and as soon as we got home I had a strong urge to call him. During my call with Pastor Maralack he said that we should come and see him the next Sunday afternoon. Carol and I were very curious about the reason he had invited us to visit him, but we agreed and confirmed the appointment.

On Sunday, 23 February 1993, we attended service at the Paarl Apostolic Faith Mission Church where Pastor Maralack was the minister. After lunch, Pastor Maralack asked us to go with him to call on his daughter, Loretta, and her husband Frikkie. They were teachers who lived in Newton, Wellington, in the Western Cape, and were travelling a round trip of 90 km weekly from home to their Monday to Friday teaching jobs in Malmesbury, where they lived on the school property during the week. They were only home in Newton on weekends. They welcomed us into their home as if we already knew one another well, even though it was the first time we had met.

Loretta then shared something very profound with us. She said she had had a dream three weeks previously in which she saw us, and God spoke to her. God told her she should give their home in Newton to us to live in from Monday to Friday, and that during weekends we were to share the house as one family. We were astonished and shocked at what we had just heard and could not believe it. I walked away from the group and stood in their kitchen and spoke to God. I asked God for confirmation. As I walked back into the room, Loretta's husband said, "You have been asking God for this, and if you say yes to our offer, it will be an answer to your prayers." That was the confirmation I needed. There and then, Carol and I thanked them for their obedience to God and for the offer to live in their four-bedroom house as if it were our own.

That was the answer to our prayer and confirmation of the eighth prophecy made by Sister Jackie about our lives. Loretta and Frikkie's home was a brown face-brick house. It was no coincidence: it was

God fulfilling His word as spoken by Sister Jackie a month ago. On 5 April 1993, we relocated from Strandfontein, Cape Town, to the rural town of Newton, Wellington, only 15 minutes or 10 km from Paarl. Besides this good fortune, God was so good to us that we were also offered free transportation of our furniture and vehicles from Strandfontein to Newton. A congregation brother in our church was a truck driver and he blessed us with this gift. Yes, God is faithful and true to His Word. He is not slack concerning His promises. Genesis 50:20, 'But as for you, you meant evil against me; but God meant it for good ...' (NKJV).[34] God will turn things around in your favour.

---

[34] The New King James Version of the Bible.

Chapter Five

Serving God and The Community

'Youth Aflame' and Community Achievements

Arriving in a rural town after growing up in the city was a bit daunting. We did not know many people other than my work colleagues and the church congregation. A week later in mid-April, we invited Sister Jackie to visit us in Newton, having obtained permission from Loretta and Frikkie to have a house guest.

Once she arrived, we spent a full day in prayer and fasting, seeking the face of God to learn more about our future. During the prayer session Sister Jackie said, "God is showing me an image of you standing in front of a great multitude of young people who are all crying out to God. God says that you should work towards bringing young people from different churches and backgrounds together as one. He says you must submit to His calling upon your life and do what He has called you to do. Lay aside all things that are not of God." (*Prophecy Ten.*)

During her stay we spent a lot of time with God and in Bible study, with some sessions lasting for more than six hours. I was very confident that God was speaking to me through the prophet.

Not long after receiving the prophecy from Sister Jackie, I had a vision with the words 'Youth on Fire' appearing in my mind's eye. I felt a strong desire to start a youth organisation with the focus on empowerment and unity. I prayed about it for a while and finally started Youth Aflame in October 1993. The purpose of the organisation was twofold: to win over young people for Christ; and to create a platform for bringing together youth groups and have them work towards a common goal of unity between all cultural and racial groups. Paarl and Wellington had a problem with gang violence and youth crime, and I felt driven to use Youth Aflame as a vehicle to address these issues.

On Saturday, 23 October 1993, Youth Aflame was born with a youth rally at the Dal Josafat Stadium in Paarl. We had many churches participating in a street march and gathering at the stadium to present a programme of praise and worship, dancing, testimonies and preaching. The day was supported by about five to eight hundred people and was publicised in the local media. Carol and I poured ourselves into the success of the youth in our communities, doing youth training, preaching and speaking at different churches, and waiting on God to help us make sense of everything we were doing and going through.

God blessed the years of our lives after that. God also blessed us with a beautiful daughter named Candice, born in 1994, and who brought great happiness to our lives as was foretold in words of prophecy through Sister Jackie. Candice is our only child and she experienced God's favour and blessings with us on this journey. Candice grew up to be a wonderful daughter doing prophetic dancing with Carol. Prophetic dancing became a part of our ministry that we believe God suggested and 'laid strongly on our hearts'.

Carol continued teaching and I ended up working as a community policing officer in Wellington and Paarl from 1994 until 1999. God used me mightily in my work with the troubled and at-risk youth in that region. I became instrumental in bringing gang violence to an end in Wellington; established the Boland Music Festival — a music competition between school, prison, and community choirs; and started a school camp project for at-risk youth. This project involved schools identifying their problem kids, whom I would then take on weekend camps to introduce them to better lifestyle choices — options for them to consider other than being a problem to their schools and the community at large. The school camps became an instant hit with the youth and I soon became known as 'Sergeant Jakes - the policeman with a golden heart'.

I progressed through the ranks of the Police Force quite fast too, while Carol continued her teaching profession. I ended up being among the first non-white police officers to help establish the Community Policing Forums in major towns of the Cape Town district and the Boland. I was also a guest radio presenter on Radio Pulpit, a national English Christian radio station, hosting a programme that dealt with youth issues and giving advice to parents on how to deal with their children who were caught up in a life of gangs and drugs. I was a member of one of the first Christian radio stations in Paarl, Radio-KC, and one of its first presenters. I presented the Saturday morning show called 'Baby Jakes Breakfast Show'.

God had great plans for my life. In 1997, I was honoured to win a community award for Community Policing in Wellington, and was nominated by the community for the Community Policing Officer of the Year award, where I would become a finalist to win the Western Cape Police's Non-Commissioned Officer of the Year award. I featured on the national SABC TV2 programme, Pasella, several times.

This could only be accomplished through the will of God — putting God first was always my top priority. The seven years that I'd spent working in the community and for the community, and being employed as a police officer, opened up my world and eyes to what the Bible described as 'the lost'. I knew I had to play a part in the divine plan God had for us as a family. Carol use to make fun of me and always said, "You are on the cover of the newspapers more than at home."

I was drowning myself in my job. Bringing change and smiles to others became as natural and as necessary to me as breathing air. I became so focussed on others and the community that in my personal life and family life at home, things were starting to fall apart due to neglect. I would always be tired, and my attention at home was not on Carol or my daughter Candice, since my thoughts were always somewhere else. Carol started to feel the 'absent dad' pressure while I thought I was working hard for the benefit of the family, not realising I was highly mistaken. Our marriage was under strain because I spent so little time at home, and my daughter Candice seldom saw me. The only quality time I really had with my family was on Sundays but then there was church to attend to. In effect, I was creating an atmosphere that was not godly and not conducive to healthy family life.

Family Reconciliation

In February 1994, Carol's mother was to undertake a church mission trip, a pilgrimage, to Israel and the USA. One day we quite unexpectedly received a telephone call from her. She asked to see us because she wanted to apologise for all the negative things she has put us through and for not being at our wedding. Carol was pregnant with Candice at the time. So we went to see Carol's mother and were delighted with the way in which God has brought about her change of heart and our reconciliation. We cried and prayed together. Carol's mother gave us her blessing and she asked us to forgive her. We also had the opportunity to reconcile with the rest of the Daniels family. Carol's brother also asked our forgiveness. Now at last, we could move forward and put all the negative experiences of the past behind us. Ever since this happened, the relationship between Carol's family and my family has been better than ever. God was good to us. We could now do more for God. Peace and unity prevailed.

In December 1994, a fire broke out in the informal settlement, Carterville, in our district. It was populated mainly by black residents and the fire destroyed half of the site. In South Africa, informal settlements, also known as squatter camps or shanty towns, are areas where people live in temporary shelters or shacks built from scrap materials, mostly cardboard, with no running water and very little sewerage facilities available. The residents live in dire and harsh circumstances. Two families lost their children, and a three-month-old baby was killed in the fire as well. I was only two weeks into my new position of community policing officer for Wellington, where Carterville was situated.

I was on holiday at the time and received a call at 1.00 am on Monday, 4 January 1995, to inform me that a fire had broken out. I immediately went to work, organising temporary accommodation for the Carterville inhabitants, gathering political leaders, and alerting and co-ordinating other relief and emergency agencies. This happened during a time when tension was high between council members and the different racial groups in Wellington. I managed to help provide the stranded residents with food, temporary accommodation, transportation and clean sanitary facilities. I acted as the liaison between the council and the community organisations and was also the media spokesperson for the police. On one occasion I was a mediator too, between the African National Congress (ANC) community activists and the council, whose members were mostly white.

Regular protest marches were being held by the black community members to demonstrate their disapproval of the way the council had managed the fire incident, leading to the police frequently being summoned to defuse conflict situations. There was one incident when the black residents took the entire council hostage until their demands were met. I would spend long hours dealing with these types of situations, ensuring that the police were being compassionate towards the community. The police were considered a 'force' during the Apartheid era, and now they had to transform themselves to be a 'service' to the community instead. This was a very unstable time in the political arena.

I was very successful in my police career, during which I worked with troubled youth and their families. The schools would call me if they had issues with any of their youth who were being disorderly and out of control. The teachers would ask me to visit their schools and talk to the youth about the dangers of gang affiliations, alcohol abuse and drugs. I would regularly have community workshops where youth and their parents would spend a day with me discussing solutions on how best to manage troubled young people.

Working With Special Interest Groups

1. Department of Correctional Services – Boland Region

Between 1994 and 1997, I was frequently asked by prison management in the Boland Region to conduct youth programmes with the inmates on self-esteem and other youth-related skills development courses. I performed my role as the programme facilitator wearing my police uniform. These programmes were implemented at prison facilities such as Hawequa Correctional Youth Centre in Wellington, Drakenstein Correctional Centre in Drakenstein, and Allandale Correctional Centre in Paarl.

On Sundays, Carol and I would do evangelistic outreach activities at these prisons with an organisation called 'Prisoners for Christ', and I later became the group's full-time preacher. This enabled me to travel around the Western Cape to minister to inmates and provide them with counselling.

In 1996, I saw a need to engage the inmates from these prisons with the community, and did so by introducing the Boland Music Festival, as described earlier. The project drew large interest and was well supported by leading politicians and celebrities alike. The competition provided a platform for people to embrace prisoners as part of their community and not see them only as criminals, and it contributed to the success of the Restorative Justice initiative of the Department of Correctional Services. The aim of this initiative was to establish policies to help ex-prisoners transition from incarceration to being active, useful members of society, and included finding ways to integrate them back into the community on their release. The initiative was also designed to allow medium-term prisoners to become involved in community-based programmes to slowly reintegrate them as useful members of society. It also provided offenders with an opportunity to connect with their victims and do reparation.

2. Primary Schools – Boland School-Camp Project

In 1995, as briefly mentioned before, I introduced the Boland school-camp project to several schools in Paarl and Wellington. This project involved getting the primary schools to identify their at-risk students or problem kids and then I would arrange to take them on weekend camps which I supervised. I organised sponsors for the camps and also received assistance from the Government's Department of Science, Arts and Culture. The camps started on Fridays and ran through to Sundays, and the school teachers were asked to volunteer as assistants. The programme presenters or facilitators were selected from the community, Correctional Services and the Police Service. The camps were well accepted and became popular among parents who considered them an effective form of help for their children. I would frequently get invited to school and community events as a guest speaker and that gave me a greater sense of purpose. I knew God had called me to impact the lives of people in our communities, and the youth in particular.

Chapter Six

Wider Opportunities

WHEN ONE DOOR CLOSES …

I resigned from the Police Force in 1999 to attend Bible College full-time, as I felt the calling of God more and more. I also opened a take-away (fast-food) shop and a catering business. God really blessed us, and I managed to spend more time with the family because the businesses were family-owned. Carol would come from her teaching job to work in the shop and we would do the catering of weddings and events together.

In February 2000, I was celebrating my thirty-third birthday and spent time with Sister Jackie for prayer. We were in prayer for about 40 minutes when she said, "God is showing me an aeroplane and a man in uniform, you and Carol are walking towards this man. On the plane I see the letters USA and I see you showing some papers to the man and he stamps them. I see a red and blue flag in the background. I also see a dark cloud hanging over you and inside this cloud I see rubbish, dirt. I sense in my spirit that you have things in your life that you need to let go. I also see you running, being chased by someone - I cannot see the person's face but you are scared. Carol needs to look into teaching positions in the USA. One of your friends will contact you to guide you into looking into such teaching positions and which agencies in the USA to get in touch with." (*Prophecy Eleven.*)

I immediately started soul-searching. Sister Jackie then shared with me that she believed it was Satan, the enemy, trying to kill the vision and purpose God had for us. She said the enemy was not happy with what God was busy doing in our lives.

It is important to realise that when you are destined for greatness and God has great victories in store for your life, that you will become a target. You become part of Satan's list of people up for assassination — you are on the hit-list of the enemy.

After the prophecy was spoken over our lives, we did not know what to do or where to start with the message we had received, but we knew in our hearts that God was at work in our lives and was sorting it all out for us as we continued to seek His face during this time.

Within a week or two after receiving the latest prophecy, a family friend named Ernest Nontes came knocking at our door. We were quite surprised to see him as it was an unexpected visit, and he told us that he had come across an interesting website, the VIF International Education Program, and he thought of Carol. Immediately this aroused our curiosity since we were reminded of the prophecy that had been spoken over our lives. Ernest told us more about this initiative which supports the development of educators globally through cultural exchange, basically meaning that teachers from all over the world could apply for cultural exchange teaching positions in the USA. The good news was that the VIF Program was actively looking for teachers to fill vacancies in the USA.

This discussion stirred up our faith and trust in God and we were beginning to understand the word of prophecy. We were marvelling at how God was so faithful to His Word and how He would position people to fulfil the purpose that He has for your life. When Ernest left, we were so excited in our spirit and we could see God's hand at work. The following day we investigated further, doing research on the VIF Program and finding out what the process was for Carol to apply. Carol was teaching at a school in Klapmuts in the Western Cape, and she loved and enjoyed every minute of her work. It was hard to accept the fact that God was saying Carol should 'take the package', that is, leave her job and apply for the VIF Program.

Not knowing what lies ahead demands a real walk in faith with God and a strong conviction to know in your heart that this is what God wants. Sometimes we have to put our own desires, pleasures and comforts aside to do God's will and what He wants for us. After all, we no longer live for our own comfort, for the Word of God says, 'It is no longer I who live, but Christ lives in me' (Galatians 2:20) (NKJV).[35] So our lives should reflect God's glory and His will, not ours.

Carol was really at an uncomfortable place in her life where she had to make a choice between that which she loves and stepping into the unknown and doing God's will. Yes, moving away from the family and going overseas is not an easy step to take but if that is what God expects from us, well, that is what we should do. It was also a big leap for us in terms of our faith — to continue to trust God to open doors and create an opportunity for us to live in the USA. We would need His support to make this transition and move

---

[35] The New King James Version of the Bible.

to an unknown place. We carried on spending time in prayer with Sister Jackie to hear words from God and to seek His face.

Carol began her application process for the VIF Program and completed assignments and filled in paperwork online. Throughout that time, we trusted God to ensure positive feedback from the VIF Program agency. Within two weeks we received a call from the organisation asking us to come to a venue in Cape Town city centre for a formal meeting with them and to meet the other applicants. We scheduled a prayer session with Sister Jackie before we went to the meeting. The prayer time was powerful as we were seeking God's intervention on our behalf.

We arrived at the hotel where the meeting was to take place and saw the other applicants there. Most of them were teachers and professional people, and there were even some retirees. The entire process looked very legitimate and above board. We had to pay the VIF Program agency R40,000 (South African Rand) for their service to place us in jobs in the USA. The process was explained to us as follows: Carol would get a teacher's job in Atlanta, Georgia, and I would be placed with a Baptist Church as a youth pastor. We were so thrilled and excited. We could see how the prophecies in our lives were coming together. We immediately arranged to pay the required fee and the following day we drove back to Cape Town with the cash in hand and paid.

On our eighth wedding anniversary, 6 June 2000, I arranged a surprise birthday party for Carol. I invited Sister Jackie and other guests to the celebration. We had a great time and at the end of the evening Sister Jackie called me aside and said that she had received a word from the Lord. She said, "God is showing me a black cloud hanging over you and the plans you have. I see a law court and you are very unhappy. I don't know what it means, but I do know it's not good. You need to be watchful and prayerful. I also see the name Henderson coming up, a tall black man, and I see chains." (*Prophecy Twelve*.) Those words gripped me. It was all scattered and it seemed out of place, a picture that had no logic. I took the words on board and made more time to pray.

It was around June 2001, and we had not heard anything back from the VIF Program agency. We were told that it would take about a year for the US State Department to issue our work visas considering all the paperwork and clearances that were involved in securing a job in the USA. I made several calls but I ended up getting nowhere: the telephone always switched to voice-mail. In the meantime, Carol and I decided she should leave her teaching job at Klapmuts Primary School, because we felt it was the right thing to do. Carol submitted her resignation and was to leave the teaching profession in December 2001. At the same time, I decided to sell my catering and take-away food businesses. We stepped out on a limb and operated on bare faith with this one.

Later in June, Sister Jackie contacted us about a dream she had had. She said, "I saw the two of you giving your house keys to a young couple, he is a pastor and has a daughter." (*Prophecy Thirteen*.) I was flustered. We had been living in my house for ten years and were comfortable where we were, materially speaking. Our house was renovated and our furniture was less than five years old. I started to challenge the prophecy and when I spoke to my pastor, Jeff April, about it he said that we should keep fasting and praying and hear what God was saying to us. Then it happened. A week after Sister Jackie gave us the prophecy about our house, I had a dream. I dreamt I was holding my house keys in my hands and as I walked into the church, I gave my keys to the assistant, Pastor Eben Mourries. I was trying to ignore the dream and the word God gave me. I did not want to share it with anyone as I was not willing to let go of my house.

During December 2001, while Carol and I were at home one day playing with our daughter Candice (seven years old), we received a phone call from Sister Jackie. She told us, "God says that you should give your material things away to a man God will show you. Do not fight God's will for your life. God's hand is upon you. You should not take anything when this happens." (*Prophecy Fourteen.*)

That afternoon I was going to the bank to conduct some business and ran into Pastor Eben Mourries while I was there. He came up to me and said he had had a dream that he would like to share with us. In Pastor Mourries' dream he saw his family moving into our house. (He had one daughter.) He also said that in the dream he saw me and my family boarding an aeroplane and his family waving at us. I was impressed by the accuracy of his dream considering that I had not shared my dream with anyone. I did not respond as I was confused and needed to speak with Carol about what I had just heard, and also needed to consult God for confirmation.

In February 2002, we finally had a response from the VIF Program agency. We were informed that we could collect our paperwork for entry to the USA and that we were to leave for the USA later that year, by June 2002. To me, that was God's confirmation that it was time to let go, to pack up and leave South Africa. By this time I had sold my businesses, and Carol was no longer employed having resigned from her teaching position in December 2001, as planned.

By May 2002, we had still not received any further information from the VIF Program's staff with regard to our departure and flights. When we finally visited their office in Cape Town city centre, we were shocked to find that the agency no longer existed. Their office was abandoned and there were no staff in attendance. The security officer on duty at the entrance to the building, where the VIF office was located on the 21st floor, told us that the VIF staff had not been seen for more than a week. Carol and I were not the only people there to collect their paperwork. There was a group of about forty people in total and we were all stunned. We could not believe what was happening — having been conned and cheated, made to believe that we were doing everything legitimately. We knew we had to do something about the situation since it was our hard-earned money that we had handed over and now we could not find or locate anyone linked to the programme. It was bizarre.

The group decided to do surveillance and stake out the office building because the security officer told us that the VIF Program agency had neither emptied their office of furniture, nor indicated their intention of vacating the premises and ending their lease. Having been a police officer, I decided it was time for some police detective work — an investigation to find out what was going on. Among the group was a retired chief of the South African Fire Services and he had already shipped his personal household goods and belongings to the USA after receiving some documents from the VIF Program agency.

For more than three months, from May 2002 onward, we went back and forth to Cape Town trying to track down the VIF staff. The timeframe that had been given to us to leave South Africa for the USA had passed. We were determined to get our money back if this programme was a fake operation, and we staked out the office building in an attempt to catch the VIF staff members. By this time, we all had a gut-feeling that something underhand and illegal was going on.

In August 2002, close to the end of the month, we saw one of the VIF staff entering the building where their office was situated. Three of us men who were on our own 'surveillance duty' grabbed the guy and called the police to arrest him. This man could not tell us why we had waited so long for a response from the VIF Program agency, and why they no longer seemed to have a presence in Cape Town. When the police arrived, we found out that while there is in fact a legitimate, functioning VIF Program and organisation in existence, this was not it. The agency we had been dealing with was fraudulent — a 'front' falsely imitating the genuine agency. In summary, the VIF Program we were involved with was a scam and we had lost all our money. As a group, we were devastated: emotionally and financially it was a big blow for us. What could we do but accept the outcome — we had been conned. We could not understand what was going on, were dumb-struck and in shock. Several of us had resigned from our jobs, sold our businesses, and had given up our homes. What now? What were we going to tell our daughter, Candice? We had no idea.

The Christmas of 2002 was fast approaching, and after discussing the situation, the group decided to let things be until after the Christmas holidays, after which we would revisit the police investigation into the fake VIF Program. We could not believe what was happening and needed answers fast. We went home utterly disappointed; we were dazed and could not even speak to each other. Carol and I went back to God feeling angry and confused. We thought we were doing the things that God had outlined in His words given to us via prophecy. We fasted and prayed for four days straight. We wanted to hear from God; we needed to hear from God.

... Another Door Opens

In January 2003, we made contact with a family friend and this lead to us receiving a phone call from a teacher friend of Carol's, Elize Minnaar. She was in a teaching position in the USA arranged through the genuine VIF Program organisation, and had heard from our friend Ernest that Carol was interested in the VIF Program as well, and wanted to teach in the USA. We were not sure what to make of it all. Elize gave Carol information to research and contacts to use to investigate the VIF organisation in the USA. Apparently, they were actively recruiting South African teachers for three-year teaching contracts to work in North Carolina, USA. We were very sceptical seeing that we had just lost a large amount of money, namely R40,000. At that stage, I had started working at the local Christian radio station as a part-time presenter and was doing catering contracts as well. Carol was at home taking care of Candice and our home, while we were waiting on God to come through for us.

At the end of January 2003, we received a call from Sister Jackie. She wanted to share a dream she had had which delivered a prophetic word from God for us. We finally met up, and she said, "I had a dream that you were standing under a dark, black cloud and that a light is shining above it. You are running towards the light. God is saying that you need to hang in there as this is a test and you are moving towards passing the test of faith. You should not give up hope, since things are busy falling into place as God intended. There is great joy awaiting you as a family.

"I also saw a big, black man that will come with you on your way. He is an African man. He will play a very important part in your journey. God is also showing me the name Henderson, twice. I am not sure if it's a person's name or something else, but God is saying hold on and you will see the hand of God at work. Pastor, you will go through a very difficult trial but it is part of your training for your ministry. God is showing me an image of you standing in a big auditorium filled with men and their wives, and it looks like a man wearing a purple robe – I think they call him 'bishop', and he is shaking your hand. I see the number 20,000 and think that is the number of people in that room. I also see big screens in the ceiling of that room." (*Prophecy Fifteen*). We needed that message so badly because we were at a crossroad where we had to get direction and we were willing to grab on to every promise received from God.

A week later, Carol called and spoke with Elize Minnaar in North Carolina, and Elize confirmed the validity of the VIF Program for teachers that she had referred Carol to. That was the confirmation we needed to start trusting again. Carol worked on getting all her paperwork together and sending it off. By May 2003, we received news that Carol had been accepted into the teacher exchange programme and had to attend a few interviews in person with the American delegation coming to South Africa to meet the candidates. We were happy again.

By the end of May 2003, I had met with Pastor Eben Mourries, the assistant pastor at our church because he was waiting for my response to the dream he told me about in which we were giving our house to him, as prophesied. The negotiations went smoothly and within weeks it was all settled, Pastor Eben would be moving into our home when we departed for the USA.

On 6 June 2003, we met the USA delegates and we discovered that the fake VIF Program was orchestrated by a teacher who had been on the USA VIF Program two years before. He had appropriated their concept with the intention of making money by exploiting vulnerable people. The genuine VIF Program is a free, not for profit initiative, and teachers do not pay to participate in it. The programme covers all expenses for the teachers and their families.

This was God's hand at work. The process went very well and within two months of the meeting, Carol received her letter of appointment. The only part of the process remaining was to obtain the necessary visas and for our accommodation in the USA to be arranged and finalised. We were told that this could take about three months to do. We were willing to wait as we had by now seen the hand of God at work. When we examined the paperwork, we noticed that Carol had been appointed to a school in Henderson, North Carolina. Carol and I also did some research and found that the church congregation where we were going to share in fellowship was under the care and leadership of Pastor Myron Henderson. That was no coincidence.

At this time, I was still not welcome at Carol's mother's house. It was not until later in August 2003, as mentioned earlier, that Carol's mother called her to make peace with us and ask our forgiveness. We were so happy that God was setting matters right in our lives. We were very pleased with what God was doing and decided it was time to move back to Mitchells Plain and spend quality time with our families before our departure. We left Paarl in October 2003, and would spend the next eight months living with family and friends in Cape Town. We left everything in Paarl as instructed by God, and only took our suitcases with us. We were at the centre of God's will for our lives. It was an amazing feeling.

By February 2004, we were living in three homes, sharing accommodation in turn at Carol's brother's home, her Mother's home, and her sister's home. We were simply happy to be spending time with our families. Then later that month, we received news that our visas could not be issued due to new USA Federal laws put into effect after the 2001 terrorist attacks. We felt like people caught up in a never-ending roller-coaster ride. Our families could not understand what was going on but we continued to believe that God would not bring us this far simply to abandon us. We trusted God wholeheartedly to work things out for us. Then in April 2004, we received our visas and flight tickets to the USA. This was the best time of our lives — seeing God at work on our behalf.

Matters Go Awry

On 4 July 2004, we departed South Africa bound for North Carolina, USA. On arrival we were greeted by representatives from the VIF Program, as well as Elize Minnaar and her husband, Clive Minnaar. Carol went to arrange her leased car and attended a meeting at the VIF offices in North Carolina, while Candice and I were taken home with Clive and Elize to spend the week at their house in Fayetteville, North Carolina. Clive and Elize played a very important part in this period of our lives. They provided sound advice as to the do's and don'ts of teaching and interacting with youth in the USA. I received a list of 'warning signals and potholes' to watch out for which would help us on our new journey.

At the end of the week we travelled to the small city of Henderson, the county seat of Vance County, North Carolina, to meet up with Carol and be taken to our rented apartment. Everything had been arranged by the VIF Program staff. We were so blessed and God was so good to us. Carol would be teaching at L.B. Yancey Elementary School, Henderson. A week later, we met the church community and Pastor Myron Henderson Sr. It was like a dream come true. I became an associate pastor of the New Life Church of God in Christ, in Henderson. I also started working in a teaching position at the Western Vance High School for troubled teens, in Vance County.

I became very involved in the Henderson community. God blessed us. I was asked to coach the under-twelve soccer team at the Henderson Community Centre three nights a week and on Saturdays. Candice would accompany me to the practice sessions with the kids. It was a family affair, with the kids' parents watching the soccer practice from the sidelines. I managed to progress the team from being last on the County soccer fixtures to achieving second place.

In November 2004, we attended a conference of the North Carolina Ecclesiastical Jurisdiction of the Church of God in Christ (COGIC), with Bishop LeRoy J. Woolard as the leader. It is an annual event held in the USA and is usually attended by around 40,000 members of COGIC worldwide. COGIC is the largest African-American Pentecostal movement in the USA and globally. In 2001, I was the youth pastor for COGIC in South Africa, with Pastor Eben Mourries being the assistant pastor. It was indeed a privilege to attend the conference considering that I could never attend while I was living in South Africa. The presiding bishop of COGIC worldwide often visited our congregation in Cape Town whenever he was in South Africa, and Carol and I were the caterers for the functions associated with his visits.

We arrived at the auditorium on the first day of the conference to find it packed with an estimated 20,000 conference participants, most of them men. The atmosphere created by the music, praise and worship was electric and you could feel — almost touch — the presence of God in the venue. There were big screens in the centre of the auditorium's ceiling. Carol looked at me and asked, "Does this look familiar to you? Have we seen this place before? It seems as if we have been here previously." I immediately remembered Sister Jackie's prophecy given to us in January 2003. It was literally a dream come true. Later in the programme of service, Bishop Woolard called me up to the podium to greet the conference. He announced me as a representative from South Africa who would say a few words of encouragement to the assembled believers. When I finally went up before the audience, it seemed surreal - like a dream, quite unbelievable. The accuracy of the prophecy spoken almost two years earlier was uncanny, and it had come to fulfilment.

The next day I called Sister Jackie to give testimony of what had happened at the conference the previous day. She said that this was only the beginning of greater things to come. Later that month, I started Youth Aflame in the USA as a branch chapter, with New Life Church, COGIC and Harvest Baptist Church in Henderson, as member organisations.

At Western Vance High School I was teaching computer science, business, and career management to troubled teens who could not function at ordinary high schools. From the first day I started teaching at the school, I was constantly buying lunch for students who could not afford lunch money, and I gave money to students who achieved high marks in our weekly class tests and quizzes. I started a co-ed soccer team at the school to introduce them to the sport. Soon I became the well-loved teacher from Africa. I was unaware of the drug-selling culture that was rife at the school.

Students would come to school and spend every free minute selling drugs to other students during and after school hours. Henderson had a major teen drug problem and it was commented on in every newspaper.

A week before the schools were to close for the holidays in December 2004, an incident happened during the course of my day at school. Two of my students came to speak to me, crying and looking sad, they said, "Mister, our family is getting evicted. Our mom is a drug-addict and sleeps around with men, and we had our lights cut off a week ago." I felt sorry for these kids and gave them the money they needed, $300. I would have done the same for any child that needed help. Unfortunately, I was naïve and ignorant about the type of teen I was dealing with at the school. So I gave them the money and told them they needed to repay it after the school holidays. They left my classroom and the day continued as normal. Later that day, some of the male students came to me and asked, "Mister, did you give money to Ashley? She bought drugs and we all enjoyed it. Thanks sir, you are a good man."

In January 2005**,** I was invited to preach at a World Missions Conference and that was amazing. Carol and I ministered to about five hundred people and God blessed us. We saw God moving in people in a very real way. This was also a real boost to the start of Youth Aflame USA, with more than twenty church youth leaders signing up to be part of the Youth Aflame network. We started having youth gatherings with young people from different churches and off the streets. We created a platform for the youth to talk and play together and hear testimonies of how good God is. These programmes became very popular in the county.

Later that month, I called the two students who asked me for money a month earlier to see me in my classroom. This time I had a few other students in the classroom when they came to see me. I asked them if I could get the money back and they left the room without answering.

At the end of the day, before I left for home, I was called to the principal's office. When I arrived, I was met by the principal, the assistant principals and two more ladies I did not recognize. I was informed that the two girls that I had given money to had laid a complaint that I gave them money in return for sexual favours. I was shocked and went numb. I tried to explain what had happened but was stopped from doing so by the principal. He told me that I was suspended and needed to remove my personal items from my classroom immediately. I obeyed, cleared out my belongings, left the school and went straight home. I now faced the reality of being persecuted for doing a good deed, as stated in the Word of God.

How was I going to tell Carol and Candice what had happened at school? I had not told Carol that I gave money to the girls in December 2004. I felt even worse now that this had happened. When I arrived home I immediately called Sister Jackie Dicks in South Africa, and just as I was about to share the incident with her, she stopped me in my tracks and said, "I had a dream last night that you walked into a dark place. You looked afraid and were surrounded by men in uniform. You were crying and at one point a man had a key in his hand." (*Prophecy Sixteen.*) I did not know what to say. I just started crying and told her what had happened at school earlier that day. She encouraged me to be strong, and said that everything happening to me was part of God's plan for my life. She added that she sensed in her spirit that this was only the beginning of my troubles, and I needed to stay faithful to God. I had no words. I could not even speak. When Carol came home later that day I told her what had happened, while Candice was playing in her bedroom. I could see the extreme disappointment and sadness on Carol's face, a sight I did not expect nor enjoy. She was crying and unhappy.

Two weeks later it happened while I was alone at home. On Tuesday, 14 February 2005, at about 10 am I saw three sheriff's police vehicles coming up the driveway towards my apartment. I immediately knew it was a bad situation. I never imagined that it would be the last time I ever saw my apartment. The officers eventually read me my Miranda rights and arrested me on 'suspicion of child abuse'. I was in shock — speechless and confused. They led me out and placed me in one of the police vehicles. This was the type of scene I only ever saw in the movies. As we drove away from my apartment, my eyes filled with tears. So many confusing thoughts were rushing through my mind, not knowing what to expect next. I could not believe this was happening to me.

At the Henderson County Sheriff's Office I was escorted into a room and waited. I was not questioned, no statement was taken from me, and I was never given an opportunity to provide my version of the situation. The officers went through the process of arresting and charging me — I was finger-printed, searched and placed in a cell to be taken to court for a bail hearing later that day. At about 4 pm I was escorted to the courthouse. I did not have an attorney of my own representing me and was given a court-appointed attorney. I was charged with drug-related offences — intent to supply and distribute, supplying a banned substance to minors; solicitation; and indecent liberties with a child. I was placed on a $1.5 million bail bond and I had to go to the Henderson County Detention Centre

– the county jail — because I was a foreigner and considered to be a 'high flight risk'.

The worst part of the day was when I was escorted from the courthouse to the jail in a police car. I was placed in the back of the car while Carol was standing at the courthouse door, watching as I was whisked away. The entire time I was handcuffed and that made it worst. I saw Carol at a distance and could not say goodbye to her or give her a hug. It was devastating seeing her standing there, crying and holding on to her handbag. It broke my heart and there was nothing I could do about it and had never been this helpless before in my life. All I could do was weep and try to stay strong. I was afraid of what could happen to me in jail as it quite common that a person accused of an offence against a child, especially involving a minor, ends up dead. Inmates don't care whether you are guilty or innocent because to them the mere thought that the victim could have been their own child, grandchild, sibling or other relative, provokes great anger. Sex offenders don't last long in an American jail or prison. And here I was, being charged with these vulgar crimes, knowing before God that I did not do anything of such a nature.

An Unintended Ministry

I finally reached my destination, the Vance County Jail. I was escorted inside, stripped, showered and handed an orange jumpsuit. I felt like someone who was playing a part in a movie, being led down the corridors, passing through gates being unlocked and locked with keys, and having inmates shouting foul words at me and calling out, "Fresh meat, new jail bait." It was very scary. I entered the cell allocated to me and found it occupied by three inmates who very politely greeted me and indicated the top bunk for my use. I knew I had to be strong and could not show weakness — once again, based on what I had learned from movies. If you show weakness, you become a target of harassment and abuse by other inmates. All I could do was pretend to be friendly and put on a brave face.

At dinnertime, as we sat down in the cell, I received a visit from the guards. They handed me a Bible and said that a friend had dropped it off at the jailhouse office. No one except Carol knew where I was and that was a blessing. I took the Bible and went to lie down on my bunk; I simply wanted to be alone with the Word of God. I was now experiencing what all the inmates in the prison in South Africa were going though when I used to preach to them every Sunday in 1996. The difference was that in South Africa, prisoners did not have separate cells due to the high prison population. In South Africa, every cell block housed almost double the population that the building's design capacity allowed for. Inmates slept sitting-up at times because of the overcrowding. I was a minister between 1995 and 2001 in the 'Prisoners for Christ' ministry in Cape Town. I was now convinced that it served as training for coping with my present circumstances. God is an amazing God.

We were four inmates in the cell with one stainless steel toilet and a single light that was very dim. Just after midnight on that first night, something divine happened in the cell. I heard one of my cellmates cussing, swearing and talking to himself. He said that he was going to hang himself, and shortly after that I saw him getting off his bunk, tie his bedsheet around the light fitting and go back to his bunk. As he was about to jump off the top bunk I called out to him by name, and tried to stop him from doing what he was about to do. I spoke to him, and with a dim light shining through the glass window in the cell door, I read the Bible verse John 3:16 to him. I shared God's Word with him for quite a long time, and there in the poorly lit room I led him to Jesus Christ. I prayed for him and he accepted Christ and went back to sleep. The following day he was released from the county jail. It was an amazing experience to have led him to God at a point where he wanted to commit suicide. I was so happy because I had become an instrument in God's hand for helping those confined in jail. The other two cellmates were still locked up with me.

The following evening as we finished dinner, one of my cellmates asked to speak to me. I sat down and he told me he was going kill his wife for putting him in jail. He hated her and wanted revenge. I reached for my Bible and shared the verses that state: '... vengeance is mine says the Lord' (Hebrews 10:30; Romans 12:19). I told him that Jesus loved him and that he should think of the damage he would cause to his children if he were to go ahead with his intentions. I told him that a family can somehow survive without a father but not without a mother, and spoke about my poor and abusive upbringing. He started crying and I prayed with him. I led him to believe that God can change his situation and he accepted Christ and agreed to forgive his wife. That same afternoon he was called from the cell and was released. I was happy for his sake but started to feel abandoned.

I began asking God questions about my predicament and prayed. I was wondering why the men I led to God were granted their wish to go home while I was still incarcerated. I was unaware of the plans that God had in store for me. Later that day, the other inmates in my cell block came to ask me to conduct morning devotions for all the men in the block. The routine was that we would rise at 5 am, get ready for breakfast, be locked out of the cells, and then have to congregate in the community area where the guards could see us on the cameras while we waited for our breakfast to arrive.

The inmates called me 'African preacher', and soon I became established as the person who conducted morning devotions for the inmates every day without fail. There were times when some of the guards would come into the block to listen to me ministering. It was the best thing that could ever have happened to me, being given an opportunity to talk about my love for God and the death of Jesus to save us sinners.

A week went by and I had had no contact with Carol. I was depressed and started to feel extremely lonely and downhearted. Later that day I received a package and when I opened it, I was surprised to see I had received five Christian books, a study Bible, and a letter from Carol and Candice. It was a standard rule that no inmate could have more than one book and one Bible in his personal belongings. I immediately informed the guards that I had more than my total book allowance, and their reply was, "You are a good man and we know you are a preacher from God, so we give you special permission to have more than the stipulated number of books." That could only be God's work and I was grateful.

In the letter I received, Carol said she was trying to find an attorney to help us but had been unsuccessful. The only thing left for me to do was to wait on God and see what would happen. It was only after two weeks had passed that I was allowed to receive visitors. The visiting procedure was exactly as depicted in the movies with the inmate and the visitor each seated and separated by a thick glass partition, using a telephone handset to communicate. I was so happy that Carol had not brought Candice along with her because I did not want my nine-year-old daughter to see me in jail and wearing an orange jumpsuit. I was so happy to see Carol that I just sat there, holding back my tears as not to show any weakness in front of the other inmates.

I carried on conducting the morning devotion, and a month later the inmates asked me if I could teach them more about God and why we needed to accept Jesus Christ as Lord. That was right up my alley. I was so thrilled to be busy doing what God had called me to do, and it was also gratifying to eventually see some positive progress with my own case. Three months went by before I attended court for the first time. I met up with the court-appointed attorney and he assured me that the state had no evidence sufficient to charge me with offences against children, and that he was going to ask for more time to review the case. It so happened that the case was delayed for almost ten months.

The morning devotions and evening Bible study I conducted soon became a norm. A week into November 2005, I was approached by the inmates and asked whether I would like to have my own cell, where I could pray and talk to God without disturbing anyone else. I was very excited about this and moved into a single cell. Single cells are normally occupied by hardened inmates who cannot get along with others in a five by five metre cell. I soon started to see the benefits of being alone in the single cell and began to spend more time in prayer and reading the Word of God. My walk with God became more intense and I was closer to God than ever before. One particular day, an older man, Jack, from Texas arrived at the jail and he was allocated to our cell block. He approached me the next morning after devotion, and asked if I could teach him more about the Bible, to help him understand it better. I was honoured to do so and we developed a very close, brotherly relationship. He would always look out for me.

It was Christmas 2005, and what sadness it held for me. I was spending Christmas behind bars, after thinking I that was going to be home to celebrate with my family. It was an unhappy time but I could at least talk to Carol on the telephone. What was more of a blessing was that Carol and I could 'conference call' and have a shared call that included my family in South Africa. This process was known as a 'three-way call' in the USA. We had several opportunities to speak to our family and Sister Jackie in this way. God was very good to us despite our circumstances. My family in South Africa were completely unaware of what had happened and where I was. On the telephone it was as if Carol and I were together in our home.

Over the New Year weekend, a young man was admitted to the jail on drug related charges. His name was Nick and he was a very angry person. I was doing the morning devotion when suddenly Nick started mocking God and our faith. He was cursing and swearing and became very violent towards me. I immediately knew I had to stay clear of him at all times. Then the unforeseen happened. Three days later he planned an attack on my life.

Jack was very knowledgeable about life in jail as he had been in and out of jail for many years on drug related offences. He came to me that afternoon and said, "Watch your back. Nick wants to hurt you but let me show you what to do when someone tries to assault you in jail or prison. You take dominoes tiles and place them in a sock, keep that stuffed sock close and ready to use as a weapon. Remember not to trust anyone." I took his advice to heart.

After dinner that evening we could sense something was up. Most of the usual inmates came to Bible study except for two who seemed to have become close friends with Nick. Not long after we completed our Bible study, as I was going up the staircase towards my cell, I saw Nick standing at the top of the staircase with what looked like a leather waist belt wrapped around his knuckles. I immediately knew something was about to happen. As I got to the top of the staircase, Nick took a swing at me but because I was ready to react, I swung the sock and knocked Nick in the face and he fell down. I managed to run towards my cell but got blocked by the other two inmates. I tried to fend them off and just as I was about to swing the sock, the alarm sounded. Guards came rushing in and placed all of us on lockdown. When lockdown is in effect everyone has to be in their cells; with no contact, no meals, and no recreation time.

Within minutes, guards came into my cell, handcuffed me and took me to solitary confinement where one is placed in a dark room on a cement floor with no blanket and no food. The space is as small as a dog kennel and it is impossible to turn oneself around in it. They called it 'the box'. I sat there crying and asking God for help, feeling extremely helpless. These were things that until then, I had only ever seen on TV and in movies.

About an hour later, one of the guards, whom I had gotten close to as a brother in Christ, came to see me in 'the box'. He said that the guards witnessed the fighting in the cell block as recorded on the surveillance cameras, and knew I was not the one who started the fight. He also said he had contacted my wife to inform her that I was in 'the box' but that I was okay and that he would look after me. He left me and I felt very safe and knew that God had heard my prayers. I was released from solitary confinement the following day and returned to my cell. I was extremely relieved but very hungry.

In The Belly Of The Whale

In January 2006, Sister Jackie left a message with Carol to give to me. She said that in 2004 she had prayed on behalf of a man in Namibia. This man was a lawyer and a South African who now lived in America. When Carol told me that I was excited because I had not been getting any positive news or help from my court-appointed attorney. In the following days Carol met up with this man at his office to discuss my case, and not long afterwards I received a call from him. He informed me that the case against me was based on circumstantial evidence and that I should not have been locked up at all. I was so relieved that at least someone believed me when I said I was innocent. He also mentioned to Carol that he was going to help us and make sure I got safely back to South Africa.

The most amazing thing about this experience was that while I was behind bars, Candice had won the award for Best Student for the Year in the county, and Carol achieved the Teacher of the Year Award for the county. God was blessing my family amidst our trial and test. Carol now had to learn to do everything herself, whereas before I was always the one who manage affairs when it came to paying the bills, fixing things around the house, etc. Carol became a very strong woman during this time. I was permitted to complete my Master's degree in Business Administration while behind bars. I received all my books and papers on time and graduated with an MBA in November 2006.

In March 2006, my court-appointed attorney came to see me. He said that I would go home at my next court appearance if I pleaded guilty to a lesser misdemeanour charge of soliciting indecent liberties with a minor, and that I would have 'time served' as my sentence. I argued with him about the fact that I did not solicit anything from any one. I was innocent but he kept telling me that if were to go to trial and a jury found me guilty, I could face five years or more in a state penitentiary based on the charges I was facing. That was enough to scare any person. It was like I was caught between a rock and a hard place. What do I do? The prospect of going home seemed more attractive. All I wanted was to be home with my family. I had already missed Candice and Carol's birthdays, our wedding anniversary, Christmas and New Year. The thought of being at home was too good for me to say no to his advice.

Two days later I had my court appearance. The attorney arrived with papers for me to sign. I neglected to read every word in the document because I was so consumed with the thought of going home to see my wife and daughter that nothing else mattered. The moment of truth came, and I was led into court before the judge. As I stood there I could see that Pastor Henderson and two of my teacher friends from the school were there to support me. I was finally asked to stand and the judge rendered his sentence, saying, "You have accepted a plea of soliciting indecent liberties with a minor and therefore I sentence you to a further six months in a state penitentiary and you will not be allowed early release. You will be handed over to the Department of Homeland Security for deportation at the end of your sentence in September 2006." I immediately became very angry. I grabbed my attorney while being handcuffed and started screaming at him, "What liberties? What just happened?" I could not believe what I was hearing. I thought I had signed a document to be released to see my family but here I was being sent further away from them to a prison. I was restrained by the court officers and the judge ordered me to be taken away to the cells. I was furious, numb and confused. What just happened? Again, these were scenes I was accustomed in seeing in movies, not ones having me in them. I was so upset I could not speak.

I was finally placed back in the holding cell. I started talking to God, filled with so much anger and frustration, and I vented. I kept on asking God how this could be happening to me. I needed a miracle but it never came. After about 15 minutes I calmed down to such an extent that the guard came to check up on me to make sure that I was not trying to hurt myself. The time I spent in that holding cell felt like eternity. Eventually I just sat there, staring at the ceiling in a daze.

About three hours later the guards came to collect me to transport me back to the county jail. I knew I was going to be there for only a short while. On the way back to the jail, the officers told me that I would be transferred to the state prison that very evening at midnight. I arrived back in the cell block and all the inmates wanted to hear what the outcome was. When I shared my verdict with them they were all very vocal in their disappointment. They said that the only reason the court sent me to prison was so that the prosecutor could justify the length of time I had already been incarcerated and my eventual deportation to South Africa. I also found out from one of the guards that the assistant district attorney was up for promotion and that this case was to be his ticket to success. In America, prosecutors or assistant district attorneys are promoted based on the number of conviction they secure. The lady who had served as prosecutor in my case was up for a big promotion too, and rumours were going around that she needed to win this case, even if it was by means of a plea bargain. I finally had to make peace with myself and accept that I had become nothing more that the 'meal ticket' for someone else's success.

On 12 March 2006, I was transported along with other inmates to a State Correctional Facility, a five-hour drive from Henderson and even further away from my family. Life would change for me. I was about to become one of the inmates of a state penitentiary in North Carolina. I was placed in handcuffs which were linked to chains around my waist and ankles, loaded onto a prison transport bus, and again chained to the floor below my seat. Armed guards with rifles and shotguns were constantly watching us and hardly ever took their eyes off the inmates. I could see the faces of hardened men, all covered in tattoos, seated around me. I became even more afraid as I did not know what to expect once we arrived at our destination. We could not see out of the bus windows as they were all heavily tinted.

We had left the county jail just after midnight and had been driving for hours, by now we could see the sun rising through the bus driver's window. The bus had made quite a number of stops along the way to collect other inmates also destined for the state prison. Then the prison's wire fences and gate became visible. I immediately felt sick to my stomach and became more nervous and afraid. So many negative thoughts raced through my mind.

At the reception and processing office, it dawned on me to let go and allow God to do with me as he wished. There was nothing I could do but surrender. That was exactly what I did. After being given orientation involving the rules and regulations of the facility, I was led away down the corridors towards my cell. I was allocated my own cell and that was a great blessing. I could enjoy my intimate times with God and pray without worrying about disturbing others or them interfering with me.

The first night went well because I went straight to my cell and did not come out until the next morning. That first morning I got up at 6 am and had to line up to go to the breakfast hall where all inmates in the population wing gathered for their meals. Later that day, I was called to the chaplain's office for a meeting. I walked down the corridor escorted by a prison guard, and all I could think of was, "What could the chaplain possibly want with me?" He greeted me when we finally arrived at his office, and we sat down to talk. He treated me well: not once did I feel like an inmate. The meeting carried on for about an hour and then he told me the most amazing thing. The chaplain said he wanted to meet me because he had heard from someone that I was an ordained pastor and was doing chaplain work in the Henderson county jail. At the end of the meeting he asked me if I would be interested in becoming a chaplain assistant. This is a role held by an inmate or a volunteer who has high credibility and the type of skills that could assist in the spiritual well-being and development of other inmates.

I was overwhelmed by this opportunity, and the same evening I was appointed as chaplain assistant, tasked with doing counselling and spiritual work among the inmates. I would also be responsible for the library, the chaplain's office, and cleaning duties in the areas where the inmates watched Christian-themed videos. The library, situated in the chaplain's office, was only used for Christian purposes. Inmates could sit there and read Christian literature and I would help them choose the material they needed. The library was also where I conducted structured Bible study sessions during the day. My chaplain assistant duties were from 11 am until 4 pm. I was also assigned to work in the kitchen in the mornings because of my skills as a chef. My day would start at 5 am with kitchen duty which finished at 8 am, and then I would go for walks in the yard until the start of my work in the chaplain's office at 11 am.

The time I spent in the prison was very fruitful. I saw so many inmates come to accept Christ as their Saviour and Lord. After working in the chaplaincy environment for about three months, some inmates asked me to help with the Praise and Worship team that was responsible for the Sunday church services in the prison. This soon became a routine for me. I enjoyed preaching once a month while also helping with the band and the Sunday services. This went on for about five months, after which I was transferred to another prison — Craven Correctional Institution, in Vanceboro, North Carolina.

In Craven Prison I met a young man who was struggling with drug addiction. He came to speak to me about praying with him, and we started spending plenty of time together studying the Bible and praying. His mother was a church minister and she came to visit him once, and I was introduced to her. She loved the Lord and always sent me letters of encouragement in the Lord.

Carol came to visit me at the prison one day, and she told me that she had received several calls and letters from people thanking her, and asking her to convey their thanks to me because their sons and husbands had come home from jail or prison as changed people after their encounters with Jesus and me. The men said that if it had not been for my prayers and counselling while in prison, they would not have made it. This type of outcome made it all worthwhile.

In July 2006, Carol called me in prison and connected me to Sister Jackie in South Africa. She was so happy to hear from us because she had been praying for us just a few days before the call, asking God to encourage us to contact her. She shared a dream she had had a week ago, and said, "I dreamt of you boarding a plane and I saw you in South Africa but not with your family. I kept on seeing Johannesburg and I saw an African man sitting with you in an office. I also saw you with lots of young people and they called you Daddy. God is showing me that you should submit to His will and allow Him to work things out in your life. I see you touching many lives. I see fire come out of your hands. God is showing me a date for you and Carol to remember, 15 November this year, and it may mean something to you both." (*Prophecy Seventeen.*) My reply to her was, "How could that be?" We do not know anyone in Johannesburg, neither family nor friends. I tried to argue my way out of the next move that God intended for us. We carried on speaking and I shared with her what God was doing through me in the prison. We spoke for about 40 minutes.

I was amazed at the news but was also not sure of what to do or expect next. What I did know was that if God had revealed this to Sister Jackie, then I knew it would come to pass. I just did not know how matters would play out and when it would happen.

Two weeks later, in July, I received news from Carol that she had received a call from my mother telling her that my sister, Evelyn, and her husband had been transferred from Cape Town by their respective employers, to work in Johannesburg. Carol also mentioned that Evelyn would immediately be moving to Johannesburg. My mother was not happy because none of our family had ever moved away from home; they had always lived close to my mother. This was no coincidence since we had been told, just fourteen days earlier, that God was planning to transition us to another phase in our lives. I was excited and looking forward to the next season of my life. In the meantime, Carol was preparing to give up her teaching contract in the USA and move to wherever God was shifting us next. I had no idea what was going to happen over the next few weeks. I was more worried about Carol and Candice being left to sort things out on their own for us as a family, than their move back to South Africa.

In August 2006, I received a visit from the Department of Homeland Security to inform me that I would be deported from US soil by November 2006. I would be transferred from the prison to the ICE (Immigration and Customs Enforcement) Atlanta City Detention Center in Georgia. Things became more and more difficult to bear as I was transferred further and further away from the family. Every transfer from prison takes place after midnight and that is quite unsettling. The only contact I now had with Carol was once a week by telephone. I continued doing spiritual work among the inmates and it was well received by them. In September 2006, Carol called me to say that she had been given permission to terminate her teaching contract earlier than stipulated, and that the VIF Program would support her in any way they possibly could. At the end of September, Carol confirmed their flights were booked, and that she and Candice would be leaving the USA on 15 November 2006.

Chapter Seven

Back Home Again

A Slow Start

On 15 November 2006, Carol and Candice travelled back to South Africa to meet up with my sister, Evelyn, in Johannesburg, while I was still locked up in a deportation centre in Atlanta, Georgia. By then Evelyn had settled in well in her job and her new home. Their kids were attending school, while her husband was running a trucking business and working as a warehousing manager for an Italian furniture store. Evelyn also served as an elder in the New Africa Gateway Church in Midrand, Johannesburg. We were unaware that Evelyn was arranging a job and accommodation for Carol. Within a week after Carol and Candice arrived in Johannesburg, Carol started work as a kindergarten teacher at Building Blocks Early Childhood Centre in Midrand. Candice was accepted into a school almost immediately. Evelyn arranged for Carol and Candice to move into a rental apartment right next door to hers, in the Midrand Campus accommodation complex which consisted of student units located close to the Midrand Business School of the Midrand Graduate Institute.

I spent about three weeks at the ICE Atlanta City Detention Center, Georgia, until I was finally escorted to the airport on 8 December 2006, to depart from the USA. I arrived back in South Africa on 10 December 2006, and was greeted at the airport by Carol, Candice, Evelyn and her family. I was exhausted and happy to be free and united with my family.

Once I arrived back in the country, I spent all my time with my family and enjoyed being in contact again with my mother and siblings in Cape Town. They were so excited to know that we were home and we made plans to visit them over the December 2006 holidays. A week later, Evelyn asked us to meet her church pastor, Dr Bheki V. Gamedze — also known as Apostle Gamedze — of the New Africa Gateway Church in Midrand. I was very hesitant as I did not want to get involved in church affairs so soon after my release from jail. I was hoping to spend the holidays with family in Cape Town and worry about church matters later. I had it all wrong because God had other plans. We finally agreed to go to church with Evelyn and her family and see where God was going to take this new development.

On the second Sunday of December 2006, after the church service, we met Dr Bheki Gamedze and his wife, Prophet Sheri Gamedze. When I first laid eyes on the pastor, I saw that he was a black African man matching the description given in the prophecy by Sister Jackie Dicks in 2000. We could only stand in awe and wonder at the fulfilment of the prophecy.

We had a great meeting with the pastors of the church, and we shared a little of our testimony and spoke about what God was doing in our lives. We were reluctant to commit to any form of involvement in the church and were inclined to wait until after the holidays before doing so. During that meeting the pastors spoke to us about working in their youth department and in their children's ministry. We did not agree to anything at that stage but said that we wanted to pray and wait on God for guidance. We asked them to help us pray for clear direction in our lives, hoping for an indication as to what we should be doing. We had no idea why God brought us to Midrand.

We travelled to Cape Town to spend time with the family. We immediately made it a priority to see Sister Jackie in Mitchells Plain because we had not seen her since we left for the USA in 2004. We arrived in Cape Town on 18 December 2006, and it was so good to see family and friends again, especially after my recent ordeal. We met up with Sister Jackie a day later and once again marvelled at what she had to tell us. She said that she had been praying for us a week ago, and God showed her that we were celebrating and worshipping God in a big hall. The walls were covered with curtains and that we need to stay in 'Jerusalem' until God shows us what to do. I knew what 'Jerusalem' meant from a Biblical perspective. It is a reference to a place where God has you worship Him at a particular time. It is a name for the place of worship. We spent time in prayer because we wanted more direction from God. After the prayer session, Sister Jackie asked us to visit her on New Year's Eve for another time of prayer and seeking God's direction. We agreed and left.

On New Year's Eve, 31 December 2006, we met Sister Jackie as planned and knew that she would have been waiting on God for a word for us, and we too, had been waiting on God for direction. While we were praying I clearly sensed God and felt a conviction that we should stay in Midrand and see what God wanted to do through us. I also heard God saying that we should be doing the work of a shepherd. The word 'shepherd' came so clearly to my mind during my prayer time that it was hard to ignore. Normally, I would associate 'shepherd' with 'pastoring' a church, but the word 'shepherd' as revealed to me, felt more like 'mentoring'. For me the difference implied that we should be mentors to others rather than pastors at a church. Sister Jackie then gave us a revelation: "God is saying that you will be welcomed into the hearts and homes of people you never thought possible. God says you and Sister Carol will see the hand of God over your lives but it will be for a short season. I see eighteen months. I also see God directing you to impact young leaders and children without parents." (*Prophecy Eighteen.*) We continued in prayer and left after about three hours. God was so good to us. The rest of the holidays over the Christmas and New Year season of 2006-2007 went very well, and were spent with family and friends.

On 10 January 2007, we travelled back to Midrand, filled with great expectation. When we arrived, Carol went back to her work at Building Blocks childcare while I was trying to find a job. I applied to a number of hotels and eateries for a chef position but was unsuccessful. A few days later, in January, I received news from some of the student tenants that the Midrand Graduate Institute was advertising for a part-time business lecturer, and I decided to apply. The position would require me to teach on Saturday mornings for five hours. I attended the interview and started work on Saturday, 13 January 2007. This was better than not having a job. We were grateful to God for the blessing.

By 14 January 2007, we met with the pastors of New Africa Gateway Church, Apostle Gamedze and Prophet Sheri Gamedze.

At the meeting they told us that while they were praying on 30 December 2006, they saw us in a vision and God showed them that we were God's choice to lead the youth ministry. We knew this was the confirmation we sought during our prayer for direction. We agreed to take responsibility for the youth, community missions, children's ministry, the performing arts ministry, and prison ministry. The New African Gateway Church was also preparing for their annual conference to be held in February 2007. And in this way, I became the official youth pastor of the New Africa Gateway Church in Midrand.

Two weeks went by, and I was still not working and at home during the week while Carol was at work. I was not happy with this situation and started questioning God about why I could not find a job, even though I applied to so many places that advertised vacant positions. One morning as I was standing in the bathroom, after Carol had left for work, I started talking to God. Almost immediately I saw the word 'servanthood' appear in the mirror and could not believe my eyes, but as I continued to pray, I kept on seeing this word. I was unsettled; it had to mean something. I went to the Word of God and found in Galatians 5:13 the words that we should serve one other through love. I spent some time studying God's Words further and trying to understand what this could mean for me. The following Scripture came to mind: 'Whoever wants to be great among you must be your servant' (Matthew 20:26) (ISV).[36] I knew God was speaking to me. I fell on my knees and started worshipping God for this direction he had provided. The question now was, in what capacity and where am I to serve?

---

[36] International Standard Version of the Bible.

Later that morning I decided to pay a visit to the church. I received a warm welcome from the secretary, Miranda, who gave me a brief on what the church was involved in on the community front. While we were talking, I had an urge to walk around the premises and look at the building. I noticed some damage and breakage in the bathrooms and in the kitchen area. While I was standing in the bathrooms, I felt the need to do something to fix the damage with my own, personal resources.

I left the church and called Carol to discuss withdrawing money from our bank account to buy plumbing parts needed for the repairs. She agreed, and I went back to the church with the intention of serving by fixing toilets. When I arrived at the church I did not inform the office staff of my mission, instead I went straight to the area where the repairs needed to be done. While I was busy working under one of the commodes, I was approached by Miranda. She asked me not to do the repairs as the church used a plumbing company for that purpose. I insisted that I had to do this because I was following God's instructions. I was convincing because Miranda left me to do what I had come to do. I ended up fixing the light fittings and the toilets. It felt so good to simply obey God and do the right thing — serve others.

A week later, I was called in to see Apostle Gamedze. We discussed the ministry and how they felt that Carol and I were an answer to their prayers by joining their ministry. They had been praying for God to send the right people into their lives to help build the work of the church and empower young people for God's Kingdom. The apostle also spoke to me about helping with the upcoming conference because they had invited a bishop from the USA to be the guest speaker at the event. Apostle Gamedze said that he was very moved by my gesture of servanthood in repairing fixtures and fittings at the church, free of charge. He asked me to be the personal driver for the guest speaker at our conference for the duration of his stay. I would be required to assist the bishop and his wife with any chores and transportation they might require. Upon arrival, I had to pick them up at the airport, take them to their hotel, and wait for further instructions from the bishop or the apostle. I would also be responsible for ensuring the safety of the bishop and making sure he felt welcome and comfortable.

This was a great task and I was excited to be chosen for such an assignment. I knew that when you embark on a mission to serve, it could come in many forms. I wanted to remain faithful. I saw life from the perspective that I needed to repay God for all He had done for me. God had blessed us in such a great way and all I wanted to do was to be of service to others and extend the Kingdom of God here on earth.

In February 2007, the Africa Arise-07 conference finally arrived. I collected the bishop and his wife from Oliver Tambo International Airport in Johannesburg, and took them to their hotel in Pretoria. It was a very humble assignment but I loved every minute of it. On the third day of the conference, I went to collect the bishop after breakfast, and once I arrived he asked to speak to me. He said that he admired my level of servanthood and that he believed that this was the start of great things for me in the area of serving others. He prayed for me and we departed, driving directly to the conference. He spoke to me, encouraging me to carry on doing the will of God.

On the last day of the conference, the church leadership had a meeting with the bishop. During the meeting, the bishop called me and Carol to join them. The bishop addressed the leaders and said, "I have never seen someone so committed, so dedicated to serving God and His people, and a person who would go the extra mile for excellence. Let me say to you: he who takes care of God's business will find that God will take care of their business." I was moved and humbled. I stood there, holding Carol's hand and wept realising that this could only be done by the grace of God. The bishop and pastors laid their hands on us and prayed for us as a family. I spoke to the bishop about my wrongful imprisonment and he suggested I contact an organisation in New York called The Innocence Project,[37] and ask them to reopen my case and see what they could do to have me exonerated.

The conference was over and I was back at home, still with a job only on Saturday mornings. I needed a better job soon. I knew all I had to do was remain faithful to the affairs of God and His kingdom and all other things would fall into place. Later that week, I decided to file a claim of innocence with The Innocence Project in New York, USA, to have my name cleared and my conviction overturned. I also filed a motion for wrongful conviction. I received a reply within a week to inform me that they would place my case in their queue but that it was assigned a low priority because I no longer resided in the USA and they were obliged to focus first on American citizens who were still incarcerated. They would keep me informed and the matter could take years.

---

[37] The Innocence Project, founded in 1992 by Peter Neufeld and Barry Scheck at Cardozo School of Law, exonerates the wrongly convicted through, inter alia, DNA testing, and reforms the criminal justice system to prevent future injustice. URL: www.innocenceproject.org.

Rewards For Faithful Service

At the end of February 2007, I received a meeting invitation from one of the church elders, Jabu Radebe, who was a businessman and a faithful church leader. He and his wife, Pumla Radebe, who were vital to the success of the church, were also the owners of a group of companies, including Bungane Group Ltd. Jabu invited me to have an informal meeting with him over a cup of coffee. During the meeting Jabu extracted some papers from his briefcase making me very curious; I waited patiently for what was to happen next. Jabu said, "I watched you during the time of the conference and noticed how well you served God's servants. I admired your hard work and dedication to serving others. I own a few businesses and wish to offer you a job, if you are interested. I have merchandisers who work as sub-contractors for Cadbury South Africa. They are responsible for the proper displays and distribution of chocolates in all supermarkets and wholesalers in the Gauteng region, as per Cadbury standards. You will oversee this division and be in charge of the picking staff at Cadbury's warehouse, taking responsibility for all activities from picking the product at the warehouse to placing the product in the hands of the consumer."

I was overwhelmed and I could not believe my ears. I had to excuse myself and visit the restroom, to pull myself together and overcome the shock. I was more astounded at seeing how God was performing a miracle for me, than at anything else. When I returned to the table, I received more good news. Jabu asked me to go with him to a car yard. When we arrived at the car dealership, he asked me to choose any vehicle I wanted and to decide whether I wanted to have the vehicle registered in my name or the company's name.

Once more, I was astounded at his generosity. It was one piece of good news upon another. I felt as if I were floating on a cloud and surrounded by angels. Everything seemed unbelievable. I eventually decided to accept the offer and to have the vehicle registered in the company's name. Jabu and I ended our meeting back at the coffee shop, where I signed the paperwork and my job contract. The salary I was offered was also above my expectation and a blessing: R25,000 per month, the highest salary I had ever earned in South Africa. That was even more than what I had previously been earning in the Police Force and the SA Navy combined!

I drove home, weeping and praising God for what He was doing for me and my family. I could not wait for Carol to get home, so I went straight to her work to share the good news. Carol was extremely pleased too, and that evening we went out to dinner to celebrate the blessings of God. The very next day I resigned from my Saturday part-time job at the Midrand Business School. Everything was so unreal.

The following day I started my new job as marketing sales manager for Bungane Group Ltd. I occupied my new office in Benoni with pride. It took me a week to get settled in and learn about the business. God was good and still is. I was in the job for three weeks when Jabu and Pumla Radebe said that they would like to bless me and Carol with a holiday to the Sun City resort, northwest of Johannesburg. That was even more amazing. Never before had I heard of a manager being in a job for less than a year, not to mention less than a month, who is offered an all-expenses paid holiday for the family. Carol and I dreamed of going on vacation to Sun City when we got married, but it never happened. And now, here was God giving it to us. We were even allowed to use the company vehicle to drive to our destination. At the end of March 2007, we had our holiday at Sun City, over a long weekend.

In March 2007, Carol and I took responsibility for the youth and children's ministries at New Africa Gateway Church in Midrand. I spent several days with Dr Gamedze, Prophet Sheri, the pastors and the elders to get an in-depth understanding of the ministry. Within six months of starting her new role, Carol established the prophetic dance ministry and had several children's programmes underway. I had a youth committee organised to help me run the youth initiatives. Within eight months Carol and I became the guardians of the Makeba Centre for Girls, a home for destitute and/or abused girls between the ages of eleven and eighteen, supported by The Miriam Makeba Foundation. Miriam Makeba, a singer, actress, philanthropist and civil rights activist, was a well-known public figure in South Africa and internationally, affectionately known as 'Mama Africa'. She was a very successful African recording artist, and included in Nelson Mandela's close circle of friends. The Makeba Centre's social worker was a member of our church.

I started using a company van to transport the girls to youth meetings and church every week. It soon became evident that by guiding us to live in Midrand, God had a divine purpose in mind for our lives. I became the 'father figure' for these girls, and Carol and I loved it. We felt fulfilled being able to share our lives, and that of our daughter, with the girls who previously knew only abuse, heartache and pain. We had purpose and a reason for living, and loved the twenty-six girls as if they were our own. Carol, Candice and I would spend two nights a week with the girls, teaching them about God, helping them with their homework, talking to them about life issues, and providing counselling. Those girls meant more to us than our own biological brothers and sisters in Cape Town. We gave ourselves to them and ensured that they were comfortable and served God. Words cannot describe what it meant to us.

By Easter, April 2007, God led me to write a musical stage play about the crucifixion, and it was one of the best things that ever happened to the youth. The play received good reviews and was popular. In addition, everyone involved in it had a personal encounter with God. The youth ministry was very successful and we soon developed a yearbook to showcase our work; it was well received by the congregation. The church and the youth were very active in serving others and the church grew rapidly.

In November 2007, we held a youth camp and had over eighty young people attending. When we took over the youth part of the ministry, we started with around sixteen youth members. The camp was the highlight of the year's events.

God continued to bless the youth and we had the best camp ever. Young people returned from the camp changed in many positive ways, and wanted more of God in their lives. We had cases of young girls being healed and restored to their parents, and broken spirits being made whole. It was the best reward ever. I soon became known as the 'Chocolate Rev.' because I handed out chocolates to the youth every week and on Sundays after church — every child in the Sunday school was spoilt and received candy and chocolates. The kids loved it. Whenever it was a church member's birthday, we blessed them with chocolates. Who could say no to chocolates?

Sister Jackie planned to visit us just before the Christmas holidays. We knew that her visit was for a special purpose and were prepared for anything. Sister Jackie arrived during the first week of December 2007 while we were very busy at work. I collected her at the airport after work, and on our way home, she asked me pull over to the side of the road, and said, "I just got this vision of you now, seeing you walking towards an aeroplane but Carol is not with you. I see you going to a place with a blue flag, the travel papers say Australia or New Zealand, I cannot see it clearly but I need to share this with you. God is saying that he is busy moving things around in the heavens and that you are at the centre of it all. You need to pray and wait on God for more clarity." (*Prophecy Nineteen.*)

After about 45 minutes, we continued our journey home. During the entire trip I had all sorts of thoughts racing through my mind. I tried to make sense of it all but, by now, I knew that whatever God says will happen, does happen. I had been on this journey for a while; long enough to know the signs from God and the changing seasons of our lives. I was excited, anticipating what God had in store for us as a family. We were very happy and successful in our ministry at New Africa Gateway Church and, even if God did not move us somewhere else, we would be content with what God wanted from us in Midrand.

We arrived home and had a wonderful time around the dinner table. Sister Jackie said we should spend the evening in prayer because she believed God was making plans for us, and that there were greater things awaiting us somewhere overseas. We made sure all the telephones were switched off so that we were not disturbed, and were looking forward to an encounter with God and the Holy Spirit. The prayer session lasted well into the early hours of the next morning. During the prayer, I heard God telling me that we needed to prepare ourselves for more greatness on our journey. I wanted to know more. Many times we need greatness to be a huge event in our lives and visible to others. God sometimes, if not most of the time, works in the stillness, discreetly, and not in front of spectators. We walk by faith, not sight; that is what God works with: our faith in His ability to complete good works in us that will ultimately affect the people around us.

The following morning, we all slept late and went out to have lunch. During our outing to the mall, I ran into Dr Gamedze and some of the church members. I introduced Sister Jackie to them and that started a divine event we did not expect. The day went well and we were invited to Dr Gamedze's house for tea that evening. When we arrived, Dr Gamedze introduced his wife, Prophet Sheri, to Sister Jackie. As soon as they met Sister Jackie said, "I just had a vision from God about you and the pastor. I see that God is going to allow a divide in the church because Pastor Gamedze needs to make right some wrongs in certain areas of his life and with other people. You have a jacket hanging in your closet - a brown, leather jacket that somebody gave to Pastor some time ago. God says you need to get rid of it because there is something demonic about the jacket. God says that the divide He is allowing is to purify the church." (*Prophecy Twenty.*)

Prophet Sheri was in tears almost at once. She got up, left the room and returned a few minutes later with the jacket — it was exactly as described by Sister Jackie a few moments before. Now that was something exceptional. None of us had ever been further than the lounge of the pastor's house and would have no idea what was in their private rooms, let alone their closet. Only God could reveal that. The evening continued and we had a wonderful time because God was revealing Himself to us.

Our next Sunday service went well and God manifested Himself to us in the service. We encountered God in a very real way and it was indeed a blessing. That afternoon, the unexpected happened. At about 5 pm, we had the youth both from the community and the church congregation lining up at our apartment, wanting a word from the Lord about their lives through the prophet, Sister Jackie. Word had gone out that God had sent her to deliver a word from God for some of the people in the church. Carol and I had to set aside Candice's room for Sister Jackie's prayer encounters with the church members. It looked like a doctor's surgery with people lining up for consultations. It was amazing how God revealed Himself to some of them. I remember one couple who were not sure about their relationship and after praying and receiving a word from God, they left more certain about God's will for their lives. God revealed hidden truths about some people that only God could know, and Sister Jackie would tell them exactly what was going on. That impressed most of the people. Here was a stranger, with no connection to them at all, revealing truths about their personal lives, ones that only God could know because He is the all-knowing God. He knows our deepest secrets.

The following two weeks of Sister Jackie's stay were filled with appointments and prayer engagements, to the extent that she had little time to visit with us as a family. On the last day of her stay we managed to get some time with her. During our all-night prayer session, God gave a little more direction to us regarding timeframes. God gave us a date to remember, namely Mother's Day. We knew what it meant but were unsure of the prophetic significance of the date. The most important thing for us was to trust God with every detail of our lives. God continued to speak to us and gave Sister Jackie another prophecy for us. She said, "God is showing me that you will influence the lives of people of other cultures. You will wear clothing that you are not used to. You will be a blessing to other men, and young people will enjoy the food that you will cook for them. You must remain true and faithful to God in everything you do. Do not lean on your own understanding, but put all your trust in the Lord Jesus Christ". (*Prophecy Twenty-One.*)

We ended the year on a very high note, when Carol and I decided to host a Christmas event for the Makeba girls. They had not had a Christmas celebration for more than five years, we were told by the staff at the centre. God laid it on my heart to make Christmas special for them. God blessed us so much. We received gifts, sponsorships and finance to bless the girls and their families. The event was a great highlight for the girls. We felt blessed to have played a part in the girls' happiness.

January 2008 started in a very pleasant way. Carol and I spent more time in the presence of God as we now knew that God was busy shifting our lives about again. At the end of January, Cadbury South Africa held their annual awards conference in Zimbabwe. This event was held to honour sales staff for their great achievements. I was nominated in a category, and won the Most Improved Sales Person of 2007 award because I had exceeded my sales target by more than 95%. This was a great achievement for me. I was so blessed by God.

Setting Off Again

At the end of January 2008 I had a dream. I dreamt that I was waving a flag and it had stars on it. I also saw myself standing on a hill and shouting, "Praise God". I did not know what the dream meant but was determined to pay attention to it. That evening I came home and asked Carol whether she would like to move to Australia to have a better teaching job. Carol's reply was, "Maybe, but let's look at what's on offer and pray about it."

I immediately started doing research and discovered that for us to move to Australia, we would need to gain a certain amount of points based on a list of criteria formulated by the Australian authorities, and obtain an appropriate visa. I was a bit disappointed but then I came across another option, namely New Zealand, where at that time, we did not need a visitor's visa before arrival and did not need to gain points to be eligible for immigration. I started to investigate New Zealand as a possible emigration destination for us. I also noticed that the flags of New Zealand and Australia are very similar and had a connection to my dream. About a week later, I went to speak to Jabu Radebe and told him about my interest in wanting to move to New Zealand. He was very encouraging and then he offered to bless me with the airfare and a week of paid leave. I was completely astonished at his generosity. The arrangements were made, flights paid, and soon all I had to do was arrange my accommodation.

I contacted Sister Jackie about the dream I had had and my plans for a life in New Zealand. She told me to stay prayerful and wait on God to confirm everything, and not to make any hasty decisions. Sister Jackie then mentioned that she had a prayer partner, Sister Elizabeth Edwards, who had two sons living in New Zealand, and that they might assist me with accommodation. Within a week we had everything arranged in New Zealand. The plan was that I would go on my own while Carol would be praying for God to confirm things. I made contact several times with Jonathan Edwards, Sister Elizabeth's eldest son in Auckland, New Zealand, and had everything finalised. I finally left for New Zealand, on my own, in the third week of February 2008. Sister Jackie came to stay with Carol and Candice in my absence, and they would spend that time in prayer and waiting on God's response.

I arrived in New Zealand, and the very next day I saw an advertisement in the local newspaper that caught my attention: a vacancy existed for an ex-police officer to do security work. I called immediately and was invited for an interview the following day. I was extremely fortunate since I had only just arrived in the country and was already on my way to a job interview. I was armed with my certificates from the South African Police Force and other necessary documents. At the interview venue I was greeted by a very friendly gentleman, and within 15 minutes I was signing a job offer and an employment contract. I was very impressed by how quickly I was offered a job, considering that I was a foreigner on a visitor's visa. I believed it could only be God making all these great things happen in our favour. The only thing that I apparently had to do was submit the job offer, employment contract, and visa application to the Immigration NZ Department to obtain a work permit. I decided not to submit the documents in New Zealand but rather at the New Zealand High Commission Office in Pretoria, South Africa. I left New Zealand three days after that and had been there for about a week.

I arrived back in South Africa on 3 March 2008, and headed straight to the New Zealand High Commission office in Pretoria, to submit my application for a visa and a work permit. I returned to work and handed in my resignation. The following three months would be a waiting game until I received a reply from the New Zealand High Commission. I was told that the process for the visa application would take three months. At the end of March 2008, I called the New Zealand High Commission to check on the progress of my application. I was told that no one had seen the paperwork I submitted and that I needed to re-apply. That would be a big problem because the original job offer and contract were included as part of my application since the Immigration NZ office at the New Zealand High Commission does not accept photocopies of contracts or other important and official documents. I was dumbstruck by the incompetency of the administration at the High Commission. I immediately contacted a lawyer friend of mine to seek advice. He called the Immigration NZ office in Pretoria, and an hour later I received a call to say that they had located my application and documents. I decided to collect my paperwork from the New Zealand High Commission, take my chances and submit the application and supporting documents to the Immigration NZ office in New Zealand, after I arrived in the country.

Carol and I had finally decided to pack our bags and prepare for our departure to New Zealand. We wanted to get there as soon as possible. The New Africa Gateway Church had also released us from our responsibilities and we were finishing up at our respective jobs at end of April 2008. The remaining time was spent selling our furniture and getting things sorted to spend a little time with the family in Cape Town before our departure. We had everything finalised by 30 April 2008, and left for Cape Town. God had miraculously come through for us with the air tickets.

We arrived in Cape Town on 3 May 2008, and had enough time to spend with family and friends, and with Sister Jackie Dicks and her family. When we looked at the calendar, we realised that we would be departing South Africa on the evening of Mother's Day, the very date that God gave me to remember in December 2007. It was amazing the way God would allow something to happen so that it aligned with the journey we had to travel. We departed for New Zealand on 10 May 2008.

Chapter Eight

New Country, New Challenges

Mighty Oaks From Little Acorns

We arrived in New Zealand on 11 May 2008, and were met by Jonathan and Nolan Edwards. We would spend the next three months with them as their house guests. Carol took over the 'mother of the family' duties in their house in Henderson, Auckland. I submitted my immigration application documents to Immigration NZ in Auckland, and in June 2008 I started working as a security guard for Icon Security Ltd. Carol had to stay at home while she was waiting for her teacher's licence to be processed.

We attended the Assemblies of God Church in Henderson, called City Church Waitakere, and were involved there for a few months. We were very well received and it was an eye-opener to serve in a multicultural church whose members were from ten different countries. The time spent in their congregation was educational but also challenging because their style of service and worship was very conservative: people would just sit in their pews and not raise their hands to give adoration to God. Our style of worship and commitment during the church service was different and people in the multicultural church were very surprised when they heard others speaking in tongues, dancing to music, and singing. Carol and I continued to pray for direction from God during our time with this church. God continued to bless us and use us in the cell ministry[38] of the church and we found that in the cell groups we could give expression to our love and faith in Christ.

In October 2008, I was offered a job as a production operator at Douglas Pharmaceuticals in Auckland, working on the night shift for which I would earn more money. That was a great blessing because it allowed us to move into our own house, as a family. Carol also started teaching again, and God continued to bless us. Later that month, I received an invitation from a pastor of the Fijian Assemblies of God Church to minister at one of their Sunday services because their senior pastor was often away, travelling regularly to Fiji for ministry and business. The church, the Living Hope Worship Centre (LHWC), was well-established and consisted of Fijians, Fijian-Indians, Zimbabweans, South Africans and Samoans. A pastor friend of mine from South Africa, Lynton Linnett, had recommended me to the LHWC's Pastor Matson Galuvakadua. Carol and I saw this as an answer to our prayers. We went to a service at the LHWC Church in Te Atatu, West Auckland, and what a service it was! We felt at home. We could forget ourselves and just let go and allow God to have His way. To us it was like being back at home in South Africa.

During the period between 2009 and 2012, we ministered and served at the LHWC Church. I ended up being the youth pastor

---

[38] Cell ministry is a form of church organisation whereby congregation members meet in small groups, generally intended to teach the Bible and personalise Christian fellowship.

and I also fulfilled the duties of an assistant pastor in the absence of Pastor Matson Galuvakadua. His wife, Aunty Lena, as we all called her, was the executive pastor when her husband was travelling and away from the church. My responsibilities included the youth, men's affairs, cell groups and outreach. Carol was responsible for ladies' affairs, Sunday school and decorations. We had a very successful time in ministry at the LHWC.

Carol's prophetic dance ministry went from strength to strength. Carol and Candice played a very important part in the ministry and their success quickly influenced the way we worshipped on a Sunday morning. The Lord blessed us and our spiritual maturity increased. During this time we became competent at performing the duties of pastors and managing a church. The experience provided us with a range of skills which would be of value in the future of our ministry. We have found that in every situation and country God has placed us, there were valuable lessons to be learnt.

In March 2009, the NZ Department of Corrections was recruiting people with policing experience to work as corrections officers in the prison system. I applied and was successful in securing a position. In April 2009, I completed my training and was posted at Spring Hill Corrections Facility, outside Hamilton, North Island. We moved from Auckland to Hamilton in May 2010. The time I spent employed at Spring Hill Prison was to become another season in our journey of ministry. I enjoyed working there because I had an opportunity to provide the inmates with counselling and share my faith in Jesus. This was a very good training ground for evangelism. As a hospital guard, I spent a lot of time with prisoners who were in hospital, and would use this time to share the love of Jesus with them.

God blessed me and that was evident in my family life. We started to attend El-Shaddai Worship Centre in Hamilton, and it became our 'home' church. It is a charismatic, multicultural church affiliated with New Life Churches of New Zealand. The pastor was Zambian and we had some Africans in the church as members of the congregation.

I was blind to the fact that Satan, the enemy, was trying to destroy this great environment God has blessed me with. I started a Bible study group in my prison unit for inmates from different cultural backgrounds and it operated for more than eight months. Every third evening after dinner, I provided teaching and Bible resources for the inmates. The other officers began to target me and the relationship among us in the unit slowly deteriorated. The conflict became worst because there were white ex-South African officers who would go out of their way to belittle me in the company of people of other cultures. To me that was like being back in South Africa during the Apartheid era. To be subjected to that kind of racism here in New Zealand was humiliating. I went out of my way to react negatively towards them and that made matters worse.

In February 2010, I received an invitation from the United Nations Youth Network to make Youth Aflame part of the global platform for youth development. I communicated online with the Youth Council and provided input into projects that effected positive, beneficial global change. I was issued a 'special permit and visa' to attend meetings in New York about youth affairs. Youth Aflame was accepted for membership in the UN Youth Council. I was elected to the executive committee of the UN Global Youth Forum for a term of five years. That was a big boost for our ministry and I knew there was a great purpose ahead for us.

Later that year, God spoke to me telling me to bring churches together to pray for repentance in New Zealand. I contacted the Global Day of Prayer office in South Africa and was provided with all the resources I needed to host the annual Global Day of Prayer, an international prayer event held all over the world, in New Zealand. Youth Aflame became the New Zealand host for Global Day of Prayer. The aim was to bring people together for one purpose: repentance and restoration of nations (2 Chronicles 7:14). We hosted the first event in May 2011 in Auckland, after networking and building divine connections with multiple churches in Auckland and Hamilton. Youth Aflame soon became well-known for unity events and rallies. We hosted the event twice more: in Hamilton in 2012 and in Masterton in 2013.

Mixed Blessings

We were unaware of God's intention to be good to us by sending a couple into our lives, Trevor and Maggie, who would speak prophecy 'into our lives' and who played an integral part in the continuation of our journey. It was as if God was gradually taking Sister Jackie Dicks out of our journey and replacing her with this couple. They are anointed and spirit-filled and always obey God's instructions. Being around them is always blessed. Our two families became so involved that I consider Trevor to be as close to me as my biological brother - I can go to him with anything and trust him with my life. Maggie is like a big sister and an advisor to us. She is a woman of wisdom and is always dependent on what God says. She would not engage in a conversation unless she believed that God was speaking or that she was being led by the Holy Spirit to speak about your life. They would continue to invest time with us in prayer and in sharing with us their own personal walk with God.

There was a golden rule in Spring Hill Prison: 'no officer should enter a prisoner's cell without another officer being present'. This rule did not bother me as no one had ever complained about an officer entering a prisoner's cell on their own. In fact, I had been doing so for more than four weeks already, during Bible study times, and there had never been any complaints about it.

One evening in November 2011, I was on duty in the unit and we had completed another Bible study with the inmates, and on that particular evening as before, there had been no issue with me being alone with the prisoners in one of the cells. But when I came to work the following day, I was summoned by the prison manager and told that he had received several complaints from other officers that I had been violating protocols and disobeying orders. He also said that one of the inmates had complained that I was "forcing Christianity on him", and that this was illegal in New Zealand. I could not defend myself. It was true that I had been doing Bible study with inmates, and yes, I had preached and spoken to prisoners about God and salvation, but I did not force anyone to attend. It was an open invitation to all - staff and inmates alike. There were also other complaints made against me, some of which were true and others which were not. I was dismissed from duty immediately and asked to leave the premises as I was guilty of serious misconduct.

I left the prison straight away and within a week, during December 2011, I had resigned from the department. During the four weeks of working my resignation period, I was brought before a disciplinary hearing committee and found guilty of serious misconduct: forcing inmates to listen to me proselytizing Christianity and promoting my beliefs in a government institution. I was told by my union representative that a deal had been negotiated with the Department of Corrections to allow my personnel file to reflect my status as a resignation and not as a case of dismissal.

I received a job offer later in December 2011, as a hospitality tutor in Auckland, and was to start work in January 2012. The downside was that I would be travelling from Hamilton to Auckland to work, but God had wonderful people and friends strategically placed who would take care of me while I was away from my family during the working week.

The attack of Satan, the enemy, was challenging at best. This journey of faith was not that easy but it was rewarding. Being dismissed from employment for serious misconduct was not a good thing to have on your résumé. I knew I had a tough road ahead but all I could do was trust God and continue to believe that I was following God's plan. I was determined to live for Jesus, and would hold on to the Scripture:

> 'Though the fig tree may not blossom,
> Nor fruit be on the vines;
> Though the labour of the olive may fail,
> And the fields yield no food;
> Though the flock may be cut off from the fold,
> And there be no herd in the stalls —
>   'Yet I will rejoice in the Lord,
> I will joy in the God of my salvation.'
> (Habakkuk 3:17-18) (NKJV).[39]

---

[39] The New King James Version of the Bible.

In January 2012, Sister Jackie Dicks called us about a dream she had had and said, "I had a dream and saw you cooking food, but the food you are serving up is not for the people you have around you at present. You need to change the spices you are using." We knew what it meant. We were going through a very difficult time at the church we attended. I was considered a 'threat' to some people at church because I was always very outspoken. I had so much experience in youth ministry that I always felt the need to contribute to the success of any ministry where God had placed us. Candice too, was always very active among the youth because of her love for dance and the performing arts. The pastor of the church did everything in his power to bring the conflicting parties in his congregation together to talk and resolve the situation. The pastor was a great inspiration to us as a family and we learnt a lot from him. Carol and I decided to play our part in the ministry of the Church and only do that which God called us to do.

The blessings we have had were that everywhere God placed us we were always surrounded by good people and good leaders. In 2012 in Hamilton, we again had a great pastor and friend who had a very soft and gentle character, Pastor Severino Samwinga of El-Shaddai Worship Centre. He was a powerful man of God who always acted in a gentle way, and he was also a great mentor.

In February 2012, our family had a setback, but praise God; He worked it all out in our favour. At the time, Carol and Candice were very involved in their dance ministry and God richly blessed them by reaching the youth through this form of ministry. I was still working in Auckland as a tutor at a hospitality academy while residing in Hamilton, about 120 km away. I travelled to Auckland every Monday morning and return home on Friday evenings. It was a difficult time; not seeing my family during the week and only spending weekends at home.

I received a very distressing call from Carol, informing me that Candice was pregnant. This was very disappointing news and most unexpected. Candice was eighteen years old and to be pregnant at such a young age could be overwhelming. This was discouraging, distressing and devastating for the family. Yes, at first this was hard to digest; we never thought that this would ever happen to our beautiful daughter, our only baby daughter. Carol and I did not know how to respond to this, and it was only the grace of God that kept us going and gave us the strength to endure.

When this happened, Candice was close friends with a young South African boy, Brent, who is now her husband. Praise God, he is a God-fearing man who comes from a lovely family. They accepted Candice as their own daughter and the pregnancy was as much of a surprise to them as it was to us. We questioned God, "Why did this happen — especially so at the peak of our ministry?" God in his wonderful way reminded us once again that He is in control of our situation. What came to mind was the verse in Jeremiah 29:11, 'For I know the plans I have for you, declares the Lord, plans to prosper you and not to harm you, plans to give you hope and a future' (NIV).[40]

We continued in ministry but at a slower pace as we had to support Candice during her pregnancy. We had a hard time dealing with all the negative issues associated with Candice's situation. During her pregnancy, Candice's faith and walk with God became stronger.

We realised that Satan was at work trying to derail our purpose

---

[40] The New International Version of the Bible.

and destiny, but we were determined to keep on going and not let it deter us. God who begins a good work in you is able to complete it. Yes, Satan thought he could distract us from God's calling through the disappointments and challenges of life, but God in His divine power has a way of transforming obstacles in order to carry out His will. It is simply a matter of how we respond to our challenges. I had to learn to accept the situation and trust God to deal with the pain and the disappointment. We contacted Sister Jackie and she was very supportive, praying with us. She encouraged us by saying that we should not be surprised at what was happening.

In August 2012, Candice gave birth to a beautiful boy, Raepheal, who is just adorable and the love of our lives. He is such a bundle of joy and a blessing from God. He is being raised in the worship of God. Candice is now happily married too, and lives in Australia. Praise be to God.

In September 2012, I was enjoying my teaching role and interacting with the teens in my classroom with whom I had very good relationships. My students were doing well, succeeding in their training, and I felt that I was making a difference in their lives. My students were young people who did not fit in at normal schools, and it was like a deja vu experience — these students were like the ones I taught in 2005 in the USA. They were students who would get into fights at normal high schools and who, due to non-attendance, were placed on a social benefits programme. They would actually get paid to not work and not go to school. That was a privilege we did not have in South Africa.

New Zealand's welfare system, until recently, was enabling the youth to shy away from responsibility and be supported financially while doing so. In 2010, the country's welfare system clamped down on unemployed youth, and made them attend skills-training courses in an attempt to integrate them back into society through employment, by giving them the skills necessary to support themselves. They would lose their youth welfare benefits if they refuse to complete the training provided to them free of charge. The initiative is called the Youth Guarantee Programme, and it works well. It is quite successful in providing sixteen to eighteen year olds with a good chance of finding decent employment.

I had a great time with my students and created an environment in which the students felt they wanted to learn and succeed. We had academic classes in the morning, and then operated a café where they could bake and cook their produce such as cakes, scones, sandwiches, light meals and more. This concept taught the students valuable business skills, hospitality skills and banking. The students were doing well and attended class every day. They were always excited about running their little café enterprise.

I would also spend time in the classroom talking to the kids about life issues, including peer pressure, negative behaviour, faith and religion, and so on. The students enjoyed the close-to-home topics. One of the students came to me one day and said that she had never before felt so at peace, and that I was like a father to her. She said that her dad had left them when she was only three years old. I soon became well-loved and my students were achieving good grades and were completing their training. I was successful in finding employment for over half of the students in my class and that had never been achieved before at the hospitality academy.

Then Satan, the enemy, came. One Monday morning in October 2012, I was having a confrontation with two out-of-control students, a male and a female. They had come to class high on drugs, and I refused to allow them into my classroom. The confrontation escalated and I pushed the door closed on them. They were not happy. An hour later, a colleague of mine, an Indian teacher who was related to one of the rude, drugged students, came to confront me about the matter. He and I got into a verbal disagreement and he reported me to the academy manager, who also happened to be Indian.

I was accused of serious misconduct based on the verbal disagreement with my colleague, and also for discussing religion with my students in the classroom. I defended my actions and the fact that I discussed the topic of religion. The academy manager formally cautioned me with a written warning telling me not to talk about religion and to keep God out of my discussions with the students. The situation in my classroom was no longer the same: the vibrancy and excitement were gone. I continued engaging with my students on the topic of their faith and God, knowing that I had been cautioned before. I could not help myself in talking about the goodness of God because I wanted to show these kids that life without Christ was meaningless and empty. I started to feel trapped and was always afraid that one of my students would report me to the manager. Teaching there became difficult.

In November 2012, I resigned from the hospitality academy in Auckland for personal reasons, to be closer to home, and to spend more time with Candice and our new grandchild, Raepheal.

Mentoring And Co-Founding A Church

I started applying for jobs and was soon invited to attend a job interview in Masterton for the position of hospitality programme manager. This location was a ten hour drive from Auckland and seven hours from Hamilton. I was not too keen on the change and was not happy to work so far away from home again. However, I accepted the appointment because in Hamilton jobs in the hospitality industry are hard to get, and I was willing to do anything to support my new, enlarged family. I wanted to be there for my child and grandchild and supporting them became my new focus.

As I was driving to Masterton for my job interview, I asked God to lead me and prepare the way for me. If this job was from God, then I would be willing to relocate from Hamilton to Masterton with my entire family. I also asked God to send the right people to me on my path, ones who would be part of God's plan for this type of transition in my life. I stopped on the side of the road in Masterton's town centre, looking for an internet cafe because I was 30 minutes too early for my job interview. As I left my vehicle, a man came across the street and I stopped him to ask directions. Suddenly he asked me, "Are you South African?" We talked for a bit and I discovered that he, Louis Witbooi, was the nephew of a pastor I knew in Cape Town, at Bible College in 2001. His mother was the sister of late Pastor Witbooi of the Apostolic Faith Mission Church in the Southern Cape, from which I graduated in 2002. We also found that we had so much in common.

He invited me to come to his home after my job interview, and when we sat down with his aunt, Mitzi Witbooi, we realised that we had a divine connection in ministry. He shared his vision of starting his own church, as directed by God, and needed help and advice to do so. Carol and I had experience and training in helping start-up churches and our passion for people came in handy for this purpose. God continued to surround us with godly men and here we were with Louis Witbooi, a gentle and God-fearing man. Carol and I have embraced every person God has placed in our lives as spiritual fathers, and they will always have a special place in our hearts.

In January 2013, I started my new job in Masterton as hospitality programme manager. In March 2013, God used me to prophesy about a few people's lives at the Samoan Assemblies of God in Masterton. I delivered a word from God to a family and everything God spoke through me to them, came to pass. Then more and more members of the church started to ask me to pray with them, expecting a prophetic word from God. This is what we love to do — being used by God to benefit His Kingdom.

In April 2013, Carol and I collected our furniture and relocated from Hamilton to Masterton, to start afresh. Candice continued to care for her child with Brent by her side. Brent and Candice would spend some months with us in New Zealand and some months in Australia with his family.

God continued to bless Youth Aflame and soon we started working with the youth of the Samoan Assemblies of God (SAOG) Church in Masterton. God opened doors for us that could not have been opened otherwise. God blessed us as we served Him doing evangelism, outreach programmes and youth services. Carol continued her love for kindergarten teaching and God blessed our careers and our ministry. We saw God at work in the lives of many people and cultures.

God blessed our connection with Pastor Louis Witbooi and in April 2013, Koinonia Christian Fellowship was born. Pastor Louis Witbooi, his family and our family had the church registered, and God continued to bless the ministry. Pastor Louis was the pastor with Carol and me assisting him. Aunty Mitzi Witbooi, late Pastor

Witbooi's wife, had the privilege of seeing her nephew follow his heart and passion.

In May 2013, God gave me a dream. I dreamt that Sister Jackie was walking next to us over a bridge. I clearly saw the bridge disappearing as we crossed. I saw an aeroplane and the next moment we were at a party, praising God. I did not know what it meant and searched God's Word for answers. I fasted and prayed, knowing that it would have an important meaning. Then a week later, I received an email from Sister Jackie. She said that she had been praying and God told her that she would be on an aeroplane to visit us in New Zealand. She also said that she needed to come to us to help us transition into a new season in our lives. That impressed us. How could she have known about the dream I had? That was so amazing. We knew we had to trust God and within three months, Sister Jackie arrived at Wellington Airport, New Zealand. We were so happy and excited. Once again, we saw God at work in our lives.

The next three months were filled with spiritual encounters Sister Jackie had with God and people in our community, and not so much with us. God used Sister Jackie in the Samoan Church, speaking 'into the lives' of many young people in Masterton. We witnessed God changing the lives of people who met with Sister Jackie in prayer. Later that year we held another Global Day of Prayer event, this time in Masterton. I reached out to many churches but was unsuccessful in obtaining their participation.

I had experienced that sort of reaction in small towns before — churches tend to stick to themselves and are not eager to work together. It could be due to the fear of losing members from the small congregations they had. At the time too, many of the churches that we reached out to for support already had their own programmes and events therefore they were not inclined to get involved in our projects. The challenges we encountered were mostly with predominantly European churches, yet God brought us to New Zealand mainly for this purpose. For us, interaction with other cultures and ethnicities was always welcomed, and it gave us opportunities to develop our ministry. It was always amazing to see how God brought people together from different cultures; sharing and preaching the Word of God together was always rewarding. Even though we did not get the necessary support from other pastors within the region, God still blessed our efforts and projects.

From 2014 to 2016, God opened the door for us to get more involved in the Samoan Assemblies of God Church in Masterton. Their pastor was a very good mentor, friend and counsellor. Carol and I fitted right in with the congregation and our relationships with the Samoan people grew. We had the opportunity to learn and practice a new culture and to be among people who shared the same family and moral values as we did; it was good for us. As we spent more time with the families we noticed daily that they were teaching us humility and love, and we shared our cultures in a very practical way. The Samoans have a warm, open, friendly and modest culture, while the Fijians have a vibrant and humble culture. For us to have had exposure to Fijians, Tongans, Samoans, Indians, Asians and other cultures was a great blessing. It gave us a better understanding of their style of worship and family life. The next two years saw us more involved in the SAOG Church, as we developed our cultural understanding and love for God's people.

Carol and I made a decision to set aside September 2016 for fasting and praying to God for direction as to the next segment of our journey. We also decided that it was time for me to complete the book I was working on and seek the face of God more intensely. I was to quit working while Carol would continue to work in her role as a support worker. I would spend all my time in the presence of God — waiting, praying, seeking and knocking on His door to get answers and clarity about our next assignment. We have always told God that we would like to go into full-time ministry for Him once we turn fifty years of age. We wanted to give our best years to spreading the Gospel of Jesus Christ. Watching the news has also brought me to tears on many occasions. It is quite upsetting and disturbing when I watch and read about the unstable political environment in Africa, specifically South Africa. I have always believed that one day I would return to South Africa to make an impact for Christ. Seeing and hearing the bad news back home: youth caught up in drugs, unemployment, corruption on the highest levels of government, an increase in crime, etc. I was drawn to praying more about the unrest situation in that country. I asked God many times to tell me what I could do to make a difference. Then it happened — He showed me the answer in Scripture.

In October 2016, God spoke to me while I was praying: "I have called you to reach the lost at any cost. I have given you authority in Isaiah 61:1 and as Nehemiah, I want you to represent me in rebuilding the walls." I saw Nehemiah 2:17 as I continued to pray and labour in prayer before God. I could clearly see a vision of 'family' in bold letters. I was not sure what it meant but I knew it was very important. I was desperate to hear what God was saying. God was faithful and during the following three months I would experience the presence of God more evidently. I had the desire to see families being reconciled to God and serving God together.

I continued to search the Word of God for clarity and on 10 November 2016, God gave me the mandate. It was locked up in

Nehemiah 2:17, 'You see the distress that we are in, how Jerusalem lies waste, and its gates are burned with fire' (NKJV).[41] But I needed more than that. I was so caught up with God and what He wanted from me, I would anything for God. I continued having dreams and I started to embrace the fact that God was clarifying things for me. All I wanted was to please God.

Later in November 2016, we received news from South Africa that my mother had been diagnosed with stage three colon cancer. That shocked us and took us by surprise. The need to be there for my mother during this difficult time became more urgent, but there was nothing I could do other than pray. The months following this news proved to be very challenging but we believe that God is in control. For various reasons, when I received this news I could not just leave where I was at in doing God's will and return home to South Africa. I stayed in New Zealand and waited on God for guidance. I simply had to keep trusting God and believing that He would care for us all.

Well, what will be the next phase of our journey? At the moment we are drawn to being home in South Africa with our family and friends, but we do know that God's work in and through us is not yet done in New Zealand. We are prayerful and believe that God in His awesome might and power will continue to lead us and guide us in the direction we should go. What is in our hearts at present, is to reach broken families and lost lives, and to continue fulfilling our purpose and calling in Christ. We do, however, feel a strong compulsion and urgency as described in Nehemiah 2:17, 'Rebuilding the Walls of Jerusalem'.

---

[41] The New King James Version of the Bible.

The months following November 2016 were spent praying and asking God what He has in mind for us next as we continue our walk of faith. We are confident that we have to wait on God's direction and for Him to lead us. While we are waiting on God we are being blessed by Pastor Louis, Pastor Pano and their ministry to help and support us in prayer. Pastor Pano Paulo, the senior pastor of the Samoan Assemblies of God Church, plays a significant role in this time of us waiting on God's will. He is our mentor and always spends time with us in prayer and counselling.

I believe that God uses any means or persons to reach souls for the Kingdom of God. I have always had a passion for people, and seeing people give their hearts to the Lord and recommit their lives to Christ is always a blessing. I will always say 'yes' to God. I will continue to commit my life and time to God, and spend my remaining years labouring for Christ, extending the Kingdom of God, preaching Christ's crucifixion and Him being the answer to all our problems. The journey for us will continue.

Chapter Nine

The Role of The Prophet and Its Impact

THE IMPORTANCE OF THE PROPHET

Prophets were seen as the 'ambassadors' of God in the Old Testament, representing God as vessels through which God operated on the earth. When they spoke, it was as if God himself spoke the words. If any recipient refused to accept the word from the prophet, they would suffer the punishment and wrath of God. To disobey a prophet was considered as being in defiance of God and His laws. Saul's case testifies to this — he was told by the prophet Samuel to do something and when he disobeyed the word of the prophet, he suffered a great loss, namely his kingship.

For us to understand how prophecy operates in the lives of modern people, we need to understand how God speaks to us and who He chooses as the mouthpiece of the prophecy. In the Old Testament, prophecy was frequently at the centre of every encounter between a prophet and God. We read in the Scriptures about the following events which took place between Samuel, a prophet and Saul, who was anointed as king over Israel.

In 1 Samuel 15:1–30 (NKJV),[42] we read,

> 'Samuel also said to Saul, "The Lord sent me to anoint you king over His people, over Israel. Now therefore, heed the voice of the words of the Lord. Thus says the Lord of hosts: I will punish Amalek *for* what he did to Israel, how he ambushed him on the way when he came up from Egypt. Now go and attack Amalek, and utterly destroy all that they have, and do not spare them. But kill both man and woman, infant and nursing child, ox and sheep, camel and donkey."
>
> 'So Saul gathered the people together and numbered them in Telaim, two hundred thousand foot soldiers and ten thousand men of Judah. And Saul came to a city of Amalek, and lay in wait in the valley. Then Saul said to the Kenites, "Go, depart, get down from among the Amalekites, lest I destroy you with them. For you showed kindness to all the children of Israel when they came up out of Egypt."
>
> 'So the Kenites departed from among the Amalekites. And Saul attacked the Amalekites, from Havilah all the way to Shur, which is east of Egypt. He also took Agag king of the Amalekites alive, and utterly destroyed all the people with the edge of the sword. But Saul and the people spared Agag and the best of the sheep, the oxen, the fatlings, the lambs, and all *that was* good, and were unwilling to utterly destroy them. But everything despised and worthless, that they utterly destroyed'.

---

[42] The New King James Version of the Bible is used for all quotations in this section unless otherwise indicated.

Saul Rejected as King:

'Now the word of the Lord came to Samuel, saying, "I greatly regret that I have set up Saul *as* king, for he has turned back from following Me, and has not performed My commandments." And it grieved Samuel, and he cried out to the Lord all night. So when Samuel rose early in the morning to meet Saul, it was told Samuel, saying, "Saul went to Carmel, and indeed, he set up a monument for himself; and he has gone on around, passed by, and gone down to Gilgal." Then Samuel went to Saul, and Saul said to him, "Blessed *are* you of the Lord! I have performed the commandment of the Lord."

'But Samuel said, "What then *is* this bleating of the sheep in my ears, and the lowing of the oxen which I hear?"

'And Saul said, "They have brought them from the Amalekites; for the people spared the best of the sheep and the oxen, to sacrifice to the Lord your God; and the rest we have utterly destroyed."

'Then Samuel said to Saul, "Be quiet! And I will tell you what the Lord said to me last night."

'And he said to him, "Speak on."

'So Samuel said, "When you *were* little in your own eyes, *were* you not head of the tribes of Israel? And did not the Lord anoint you king over Israel? Now the Lord sent you on a mission, and said, 'Go, and utterly destroy the sinners, the Amalekites, and fight against them until they are consumed.' Why then did you not obey the voice of the Lord? Why did you swoop down on the spoil, and do evil in the sight of the Lord?"

'And Saul said to Samuel, "But I have obeyed the voice of the Lord, and gone on the mission on which the Lord sent me, and brought back Agag king of Amalek; I have utterly destroyed the Amalekites. But the people took of the plunder, sheep and oxen, the best of the things which should have been utterly destroyed, to sacrifice to the Lord your God in Gilgal."

'So Samuel said:

"Has the Lord *as great* delight in burnt offerings and sacrifices,
    As in obeying the voice of the Lord?
    Behold, to obey is better than sacrifice,
    And to heed than the fat of rams.
    For rebellion *is as* the sin of witchcraft,
    And stubbornness *is as* iniquity and idolatry. Because you have rejected the word of the Lord,
    He also has rejected you from *being* king."

'Then Saul said to Samuel, "I have sinned, for I have transgressed the commandment of the Lord and your words, because I feared the people and obeyed their voice. Now therefore, please pardon my sin, and return with me, that I may worship the Lord."

'But Samuel said to Saul, "I will not return with you, for you have rejected the word of the Lord, and the Lord has rejected you from being king over Israel."

'And as Samuel turned around to go away, Saul seized the edge of his robe, and it tore. So Samuel said to him, "The Lord has torn the kingdom of Israel from you today, and has given it to a neighbour of yours, *who is* better than you. And also the

Strength of Israel will not lie nor relent. For He *is* not a man, that He should relent."

'Then he said, "I have sinned; *yet* honour me now, please, before the elders of my people and before Israel, and return with me, that I may worship the Lord your God." So Samuel turned back after Saul, and Saul worshiped the Lord'.

What we see here is a clear indication of the value of the prophet. When God gave the prophet Samuel the word to give to Saul, he did not divert from the core message. Samuel told Saul exactly what God expected to be done and how. Saul in his own mind thought he could cheat the prophet but he did not understand that was the prophet was the 'ambassador' of God. It was as if God Himself was there in the body of Samuel.

With regard to the characteristics of prophets, the article *Prophets and The Prophetic*,[43] by Art Nelson, (2004), of Life Steam Teaching, provides some insights that are referred to here. One finds that prophetic people are naturally supernatural. Their walk in the Spirit is a peaceful, natural expression of the Life of the Lord, and as different situations and challenges are encountered, the power of the Spirit is shown in a most natural way. The Holy Spirit may be manifested in a simple manner or in a dramatic, powerful display of the magnificence of the Lord.

Those called as prophets often have a 'hard core' personality — they are usually abrasive towards others. They tend to speak

---

[43] Online article: *Prophets and the Prophetic* by Art Nelson, 2004. Lifestream Teaching Ministries.
URL: http://www.lifestreamteaching.com/Teaching%20pdf/Prophets%20and%20the%20Prophetic.pdf

in absolutes without any apparent mercy or compromise. As a consequence, they experience a measure of conflict in their relationships, especially since they may be delivering messages that people are not ready to hear or do not want to hear.

Very often a prophet of God is someone who does not spend time socialising with others because they are seen as holy vessels and people tend to steer clear of them. Most times it's because of fear that their 'sins' might be revealed by the prophet. I remember after meeting Sister Jackie for the first time, how afraid I was to be in her presence. I was always anxious that she would reveal something to me that I was ashamed of. Consequently, I was cautious and made sure before meeting with her that there was nothing secretive in my life that may be awkward for me if revealed.

Heed The Word Of Prophecy

Personal prophecy has the ability to bring enlightenment and spiritual upliftment on the one hand, but on the other hand can cause damage and confusion — based on how the believer responds to the prophetic word. Carol and I have seen and experienced both situations. When we were in South Africa in 2001, Sister Jackie told us during a prayer session: "Be on guard because the enemy wants to sieve you like wheat from the chaff." The warning was spoken then that we should be on guard but when I arrived in the USA in 2004, I got carried away with the experience of living in a new country and the warning was not heeded.

I wanted to become a friend to my students instead of their role model as a teacher at Western Vance High School. I should have been on guard when the girls came to ask me for the money. I should have done the right thing by reporting them to the principal when I gave them the money to help their parents, as I believed was the case. I should have had another teacher present when I handed them the money. I was trying to do something good but the enemy used that and turned it into something very bad. I should have been on guard and have had some mechanisms in place to safeguard myself against any backlash or vindictive behaviour.

Reading the story about Saul makes me realise that when God tells me to do something, I should follow it to the letter or suffer the consequences. Saul experienced the result of not following God's instructions exactly. While the prophet is the conduit for God's message to the recipient, the prophet is also the 'go to person' for speaking to God. Moses had first-hand experience of this. Whenever God wanted to give a message to the children of Israel; He would meet with Moses and convey His word or message. He was the messenger or postman that would deliver the message. God could hardly speak to the children of Israel directly because God was entirely holy.

It reminds me of the Old Testament's Holy of Holies which refers to the inner sanctuary of the Tabernacle where God dwelt and the Ark of the Covenant rested. Only the high priest was allowed into the inner sanctuary and there was a procedure for entry he had to adhere to. A rope would be tied around the waist of the high priest before he could enter the Holy of Holies. He could only enter on one day of the year (Yom Kippur) and if he was found to be unclean or had any form of sin in him; he would be struck dead in the presence of God. The guards on the outside of the Holy of Holies would then pull the high priest's dead body out of the inner sanctuary using the attached rope.

This Old Testament Hebrew practice is a clear indication of how much value and sanctity God's presence has. Prophets had to be pure and without sin. They were considered the holy vessels and mouthpieces of God. God cannot operate through a 'dirty' vessel. There are more stories too, of other figures in the Old Testament who were at the centre of prophecy and these are worth rereading.

In the New Testament, however, we experience prophecy differently. We have been given free access to the throne of God. When Jesus Christ came to dwell amongst us here on earth, we were given the Holy Spirit to dwell within us to guide us and to reveal God's purpose for us. We would no longer need a mediator or a prophet to speak to us as a representative of God. The Holy Spirit's function was that of God himself. We serve God the Father, who is God; and Jesus Christ who is the author of our faith, the very reason why we believe; and the Holy Spirit, who is God within us.

Even so, God still anoints prophets today to deliver His words but most times God speaks to us directly and through His Word in the Bible. The prophets of today could be anyone — the pastor of the church, a relative, a friend or a stranger. The Holy Spirit, who lives in us, helps us to hear the voice of God and to see God moving though people to impact us in a prophetic way.

Hebrews 1:1-2,

'God, who at various times and in various ways spoke in time past to the fathers by the prophets, has in these last days spoken to us by His Son, whom He has appointed heir of all things, through whom also He made the worlds' (NKJV).

Revelation 19:10,

'And I fell at his feet to worship him. But he said to me, "See that you do not do that! I am your fellow servant, and of your brethren who have the testimony of Jesus. Worship God. For the testimony of Jesus is the spirit of prophecy'" (NKJV).

The article *A Prophetic Church – A Prophetic People*,[44] (2003-2007), by Art Nelson of Lifestream Teaching Ministries, discusses the role of the Holy Spirit as the administrator of the Godhead. According to the article, the Holy Spirit guides us in all truth when it comes to God. He takes what belongs to Jesus and shows it to us. Whatever the Holy Spirit hears, that's what He speaks to us. The Holy Spirit is the administrator of what belongs to God and of what God says. The Holy Spirit is the only channel of access to the council of the Godhead — he hears and brings it back to us.

1 Corinthians 2:9-13,

'Eye has not seen, nor ear heard. Nor have entered into the heart of man, the things which God has prepared for those who love Him.

'But God revealed them to us His Spirit; for the Spirit searches all things, yes, the deep things of God. For what man

---

[44] Online article: *A Prophetic Church – A Prophetic People* by Art Nelson, 2003-2007. From Lifestream Teaching Ministries' series: *The Prophetic Church — an Individual and Corporate Expression of Jesus*. Section One: *Foundation Principles for the Prophetic*. 2003-2007.
URL: http://www.lifestreamteaching.com/Teaching%20HTML/The%20Prophetic%20Church.html

knows the things of a man except the spirit of the man which is in him? Even so no one knows the things of God except the Spirit of God, that we might know the things that have been freely given to us by God.

'These things we also speak, not in words which man's wisdom teaches, but which the Holy Spirit teaches, comparing spiritual things with spiritual' (NKJV).

Our understanding of how God speaks to us or reveals His intentions to us is found in the pages of Scripture. God allows seasons and experiences in our lives to mature us and to clarify His will for us. We have been called for a purpose.

Genesis 15:13-14,

'Then He said to Abram: "Know certainly that your descendants will be strangers in a land *that is* not theirs, and will serve them, and they will afflict them four hundred years. And also the nation whom they serve I will judge; afterward they shall come out with great possessions. Now as for you, you shall go to your fathers in peace; you shall be buried at a good old age"' (NKJV).

Abram (Abraham) was given a prophetic word from God that would change the course of history forever. Abram knew he could trust God because of his faith in God. Abram ultimately became the starting point of all generation through which the promise would be fulfilled by God, to bless and increase. Abram had to surrender his own will completely unto God for that promise of blessing to be fulfilled.

Carol and I experienced that same kind of faith. Even though we did not understand when Sister Jackie spoke the first prophetic word to us in 1990, we just had to surrender our own will unto God and believed that whatever God said would eventually happen. This was not easy for us. Our families did not understand what was happening, but we had an idea that faith is about believing something even when we could not see anything of substance at the time. To understand our place in the stream of God's will we must understand the purpose of the Father and the timeline of God. All work of the Lord, which has been assigned to us, is woven into the fabric of God's eternal purpose.

As children of God, we are called to mature into Christlikeness. The process of that maturity takes time. We are taught in the Bible that everything on earth has a season and a time. When we are given a prophetic word, we need to understand that there will be a process involved for the prophecy to come to pass. We are reminded that David was only around fourteen years old when he was anointed and prophetically prepared for the kingship of Israel, and only at the age of thirty was he crowned as king. The process of preparing him for what was to come took sixteen years. David had to learn what it was like to succeed, to fail, to be tempted and to overcome.

Carol and I had gone through a similar process of maturation. We started to work with young people in a small rural town, and then progressed to working with victims of crime in South Africa, relocated to the USA to experience a different culture, and now we are doing a range of activities in New Zealand. The entire time we have spent maturing has been filled with success, failures, disappointments, temptation, negative influences and blessings. This process is ongoing. We don't ever 'arrive' at maturity. The development of a Christlike character cannot be rushed.

The process reminds me of when Carol was pregnant with our daughter, Candice. From the time of conception, there is a nine-month process that cannot be accelerated. During the nine months, Carol would experience good days, feeling-sick days, very bad days, low-energy days and craving days. Her moods would never be the same. Imagine if I became impatient and asked the doctor to remove the baby before the full term was over: disaster. The joy and excitement at the birth of our daughter is something that words cannot describe. It is the same with prophetic maturity. Once we receive a word from God, we cannot rush it. It will go through a necessary process until its birth. When the birth takes place for that word to come to pass, words cannot describe the joy. God will send people who will confirm, support and strengthen the word given. You will know for sure when it is the manifestation of that prophetic word. There will be no doubt in your heart.

Chapter Ten

Understanding the Process of Our Journey

How Do We Receive Prophecy?

Prophecy *must* come from God. It is God revealing his plans for our lives and therefore He wants us to live out His plans on earth. Hearing and receiving prophecy cannot be taken lightly because we assume that God has revealed our future. Prophecy can be revealed through the prophet or directly from God.

In the Old Testament, we read about how Eli taught a young boy, Samuel, to be sensitive to the voice of God. Samuel was growing up in the temple with Eli, his uncle. Samuel heard a voice one night, calling his name. He thought it was Eli but it was God. Eli instructed the boy to listen very carefully and that, when he heard the voice again, he should say, "Speak Lord, for your servant is listening." We too can have similar experiences but we need to obey God's voice and not question His instructions. We can do that by adhering to the following guidelines, as derived from the article *13 Keys to Receive and Release a Prophetic Word*,[45] (2013), by Michelle McClain:

1. Put on our spiritual ears; switch on our spiritual hearing.

We are called as priests and mouthpieces for God to spread His Word and will to all mankind. Michelle McClain writes, 'Spend quality time in the presence of God, understanding our responsibility to minister to God and then to His people. Worship is the doorway to receiving the revelation from God. We must develop a relationship and fellowship with the God who knows everything about everything'. We must be able to hear the voice of God and be sensitive to the guidance of the Holy Spirit.

2. Activate our faith.

We must act upon what we believe. Michelle McClain writes, 'The word *proportion* refers to a ratio. You can have faith to prophesy to one person or faith to prophesy to a hundred people. It's all based on the proportion of your faith'. In the

---

[45] Online article: *13 Keys to Receive and Release a Prophetic Word*, by Michelle McClain-Walters published online by Firestorm Ministries International. Article URL: http://www.charismamag.com/spirit/prophecy/17578-13-keys-to-receive-and-release-a-prophetic-word
Also: http://firestormministry.com/fs-prophetic-nuggets-archives/
Ms McClain-Walters is the author of *The Prophetic Advantage*, from which the article was excerpted. Charisma House, (2012).
ISBN-10: 1616386231; ISBN-13: 978-1616386238

Understanding the Process of Our Journey

Bible, Paul challenged Timothy to stir up the gift that was given to him (2 Timothy 1:6).

3. Ask, seek, and knock (Matthew 7:7–11).

Michelle McClain continues: 'We can ask God for a prophetic word. ... Jesus states that if you ask the Father for gifts, He will not give you something contrary to what you ask. God our Father, who is so in love with human beings, loves to hear the sound of a human voice asking and inquiring of Him. Jeremiah 33:3 says, "Call to Me, and I will answer you, and show you great and mighty things, which you do not know."' We constantly need to ask God for what it is He wants to say through prophecy.

4. Stay focussed.

The focus should be on what God is saying to us. We should not focus on anything other than God and His plan for us. Look in the spirit. Ask yourself, "What do I see, feel or have knowledge about when it comes to this situation?"

5. God could reveal a sentence, a word, a picture or a thought.

You could be praying and suddenly you see a sentence or a word or a picture. God speaks into our spirit and reveals Himself to us. We must exercise our faith to release the revelation given. It is like a piece of a puzzle in a big picture. God will not force you to do anything. We must speak it for ourselves. As we do that, God completes the big picture for us.

6. Be likeminded to Christ.

The Bible teaches us that we have the mind of Christ (1 Corinthians 2:16). It is when we allow Christ to have His way in and through us, that we eventually experience the power of God being manifested in our prophecy.

7. Recognize the voice of the Lord.

Michelle McClain writes, 'God drops things into your spirit, and they manifest on the screen of the spirit called the imagination. Because the Lord speaks through your human spirit, the voice sounds like your voice. It's not normally an outside voice, but the Lord will quicken words to your human spirit, and the voice sounds like you. God speaks through your personality. God will add life to ordinary words, experiences and things that you can relate to'.

Carol and I were constantly challenged in trying to understand what God was doing in and through us in our lives. God gave us clarity by reminding us of the people He placed along our journey, and the spoken prophecies we have received over the years. I came to understand that being on a journey with God is mysterious because God reveals His secrets along the way and not all at once.

Growing up as children we were taught that we should be seen and not heard. Maturing as a Christian has the opposite effect whereby we are heard and not seen. We grow deeper into God's love and become very vocal in our relationship with God. We tend to share our experiences with others and that can sometimes make us very vulnerable. We become vulnerable by exposing our thoughts and hearts to people we barely know, yet it's a requirement of God for us to be part of a greater unit in the body of Christ.

We came to understand that to be used by God and to be able to mature into Christlikeness, we need the help of other Christians. We cannot express our love for God and His children unless we are engaged with other like-minded people. While this involvement with our Christian community is required, Carol and I have learnt over the years that we should select what information about our prophetic journey is meant for public knowledge, and what is reserved for our personal use.

We had to learn as well that we should be receptive to God at all times and that it meant being open-minded about who God allowed into our lives. We came to realise that not all people we meet and encounter on our journey are meant to be part of what God was doing through us and in us. God has, however, blessed us with godly men to serve as counsellors in our lives, such as Pastor Eben Mourries, Cape Town, South Africa; Pastor Lourens Maralack Sr, Paarl, South Africa; Late Pastor Jeffrey April, Wellington, South Africa; Dr B.V. Gamedze, Johannesburg, South Africa; Pastor Matson Galuvakadua, Fiji; Pastor Anthony McMillan, Australia/New Zealand; Pastor Severino Samwinga, New Zealand; Pastor Alfred Alexander, Jabulani Ministries, New Zealand; and other brothers who would help us grow and strengthen us on this journey.

What Do We Do While We Wait On God To Fulfil Our Prophecy?

While waiting in a doctor's waiting room one can read, pray, talk, and so forth, but for most people it is a challenge to wait for something to occur. Waiting for a promise to be realised is even more of a challenge because we have the tendency to want things to be done quick. We can let our children wait when we are not yet ready to do or deliver what is intended, but when it comes to God's prophecies we somehow become impatient. Imagine buying a Christmas gift for your son or daughter long before Christmas Day, and then consider how they experience the waiting period and their uncertainty before it is handed over to them. Waiting for prophecy to be fulfilled is similar — while think that nothing is happening, or are uncertain about what will happen, or even when, we should know that God is working behind the scenes.

Likewise, when we are waiting on God we need to allow time to do the following:

1. Trust God that he will give us the best. Psalm 34:8, 'O taste and see that the Lord is good: blessed is the man that trust in him.'
   We need to understand that God is good and that he wants us to trust in him. Knowing that God is on our side gives us confidence in what God has in store for us. I know that God has the best in store for us.
2. Continue to pray without ceasing: I Thessalonians 5:17, 'Pray without ceasing.'

A prophetic word challenges us to pray without ceasing. While waiting on God's promise to come to pass we need to talk to God continually, that is what prayer is about. We can thank God without ceasing, for what he is about to do in our lives. Knowing that God is working in the background is priceless. No demon can stop us from giving thanks to God.

Attacks To Kill The Prophecy

A prophetic word from God opens up challenges from Satan. The challenges arise in all sorts of ways and forms but knowing what to do in these circumstances will sustain us. Receiving prophecy builds the character of the receiver, it requires the receiver to stand firm and become stronger in their spirit. God calls us to defend and protect the prophecy we have received by praying and being careful not to share it with others until it has come to fulfilment. Like a bear protecting her cubs so we have to protect prophecy.

According to Friedrich Nietzsche: 'That which does not kill us makes us stronger'. Challenges can turn into blessings when God is with us. Writing this book was a challenge but, through the grace of God, it is my prayer that many will be blessed by it.

Carol and I were very much aware that our journey would not be an easy one, and were regularly warned by Sister Jackie to be on our guard. I realised very early in Carol and my relationship that the enemy was not happy with our choices. Carol and I made a conscious decision to stay faithful to God and to the calling to which God summoned us. We experienced attacks by Satan very early on, as far back as 1990, and are constantly reminded that our fight is not against people of flesh and blood, but against the darkness of this world.

In 1993, I experienced the attacks first-hand when I was accused of having an extra-marital affair by one of the members of our youth at church. He claimed he saw me at the river with another woman while I was actually at a Bible study session. When he was confronted by Carol and the pastor of the church, he changed his story several times.

In 1994, while I was serving as a police officer in Wellington, a colleague accused me of accepting a bribe from a farmer. I was brought before a disciplinary hearing and found not guilty.

In 1995, I was charged with serious misconduct for contacting businesses to ask them to provide the police with a vehicle so that the officers could do their work. This happened during the time when the station commander was allowed to take the police vehicle home at the end of the day, thereby leaving the community policing office without a vehicle to use for official purposes. A member of the Community Policing Forum mobilised the schools and the community to protest the fact that a white police officer could take a police vehicle home while policing was suffering and services were not being rendered to the community. This led to a political unrest situation in Wellington — all the teachers and high schools held a protest march outside the police station in 1995 to demand the resignation of the white police station commander, and the appointment of a non-white police commander.

In 1997, I was the subject of a police investigation into theft of a police motor vehicle. I was working at the Police Commissioner's Office as a management consultant to the Area Commissioner. I was in disagreement with a white female officer about a certain process, and she targeted me in a vindictive manner. The background to this was that I was involved in a community youth project and the female officer had a hatred for non-white people. She and I frequently argued about race-related issues, and the police's role in going the extra mile to win the trust of the community. On one occasion I was assigned a police vehicle to use for a community project involving black residents. This woman had an issue with me using a police vehicle to help the black residents. She laid a charge against me of theft of a police vehicle and unauthorised use of a police vehicle. I was brought before the Commissioner of Police and was found to be not at fault. The complaint was dismissed.

The attacks would not end there. I have a strong character and can come across as very assertive, and to some people that is overwhelming. In most of my employment situations, I was always seen as a threat and a confrontation was never far behind. In most cases, the conflict involved a white person. I remember in 2007, when I was working for Cadbury South Africa as a sales representative, there was a white man who had an issue with my assertiveness. He went out of his way to make my period of employment uncomfortable for me.

Experiencing the events described above, and then later the wrongful imprisonment in the USA, led me to understand that we will be attacked and slandered during our journey with God. We just need to keep going and carry on believing that God is our master and mediator. I have also come to realise that whatever anyone says about me, as long as I live my life to honour God and live according to his teachings, the negative perceptions will eventually fade.

Stand Strong In Your Faith: During The Battle And The Attacks

There are many ways to counter the attacks of the enemy and his attempts to kill our prophecy. We are reminded in the Word of God, Ephesians 6:10–20, to put on the full armour of God. We are to be fully clothed for warfare. I am reminded of the time when I was serving in the South African Navy — we had to dress appropriately for every occasion. When we held defensive manoeuvres and combat sea operations involving other naval vessels, all personnel were required to wear battle gear and man their battle stations; as if we were at war at sea. I was dressed in battle gear which consisted of a fireproof overall, a breathing mask and a bullet-proof vest. I was responsible for handling a 7.65 mm naval artillery gun on the ship. I was not allowed to move from my post, even if I had to use the toilet; it was not allowed. The safety of the other crew on the ship was at stake. When I served in the South African Police, I had to wear a bulletproof vest, riot gear, be armed with an R1 Battle Rifle, a 9 mm handgun and a pump-action shotgun. All this gear was necessary to equip me for any form of violent confrontation.

Imagine if I were to go into these dangerous situations dressed in an office suit and tie, shiny shoes and a briefcase. I would have been the laughing stock of the officers, my crew and colleagues — and I would have been killed by the enemy.

Jesus Christ too, expects His followers to be suitably dressed and armed when they are being attacked by Satan, our enemy. We should be dressed from head to toe as follows (Ephesians 6:14-17) (paraphrased): The head is covered with the helmet of salvation, the chest area covered with the breastplate of righteousness, the waist is girded with truth, the feet are protected by the preparation of the Gospel, in one of our hands we hold the shield of faith, and in the other hand we wield the sword of the Spirit — which is the Word of God. As you can gather, in the spiritual battle we should be fully protected and safe.

Here are a few more Bible verses to help you stand firm and be strong when you are attacked:

1. 'Therefore, submit to God. Resist the devil, and he will flee from you' (James 4:7) (NKJV).[46]

Submit here means to place oneself under the control of another person or authority. The proud person will find this to be an ultimate challenge. Those unwilling to submit to the control of God and His power will never experience the grace that God promises His children. We cannot beat the devil with only our own strength. We need God's grace and power to do that. Humble submission to God's grace and power will give us the ultimate victory.

2. 'You are of God, little children, and have overcome them; because He who is in you, is greater than he who is in the world' (1 John 4:4) (NKJV).

We have a status and victory which is found in Christ. Regardless of the opposition, attacks, false teachers, accusations against us, and pressures of this world, we have the assurance that God who lives in us is much greater and stronger than all of these combined. We don't need to fear what anyone thinks of us or what they do to us. God will always have our backs.

3. 'For though we walk in the flesh, we do not wage war according to the flesh. For the weapons of our warfare are not carnal but mighty in God for pulling down strongholds, casting down arguments and every high thing that exalts itself

---

[46] All Scripture in this section is from the New King James Version of the Bible unless otherwise indicated.

against the knowledge of God, bringing every though into captivity to the obedience of Christ' (2 Corinthians 10:3-5) (NKJV).

The Christian is armed with spiritual weapons rather than worldly wealth, personal power or strategic strength. Warfare that successfully demolishes strongholds is conducted with faith and obedience, fortified by the work of Christ and empowered by the Holy Spirit. In every culture, God's soldiers will have to defend the truth against attacks, battling the arguments that deny or reject the knowledge of God. Christians must be sure that their measuring stick for all claims of truth is the surety of divine revelation rather than the false security of human reason. Any teaching that exalts itself against the knowledge of God *must* be cast down and destroyed.

4. 'Be sober, be vigilant, because your adversary the devil walks about like a roaring lion, seeking whom he may devour. Resist him, steadfast in the faith, knowing that the same sufferings are experienced by your brotherhood in the world' (1 Peter 5:8-9) (NKJV).

Satan, the real enemy and the accuser of Christians, has a way of getting people to blame each other and blame God for their sufferings. Peter writes here that Satan is like a half-starved lion in his restless hunger to find, defeat and devour God's children, especially in times of suffering. Satan will do anything to make us weak and make us feel 'useless' so that we could blame God. No one should ever under-estimate the devil. God is greater and more powerful than Satan. When we resist Satan in the power of the Holy Spirit, he will flee.

5. "'No weapon formed against you shall prosper; and every tongue which rises against you in judgment you shall condemn. This is the heritage of the servants of the Lord, and their righteousness is from Me," says the Lord' (Isaiah 54:17) (NKJV).

We have the assurance that no matter what plan or attack the enemy launches against us, we have the power and authority, given by God Himself, to overcome the attacks. We have power of life and death in our tongue and when we speak, we create. God has given us creative power. We can hurt a person by the things we say to them or we can bring healing and a smile to someone by our words. We should always be mindful of what we say to others. We can destroy the negative words people speak to us by believing that we are 'overcomers' in Christ Jesus.

6. 'Yet in all these things, we are more than conquerors through Him who loved us (Romans 8:37) (NKJV).

The word 'more than conquerors' is derived from the Greek word *hupernikomen*. *Nike* means to 'overcome', *huper* means 'over and above'. When put together they mean 'over and above'. We have victory that is over and above our own human strength. It is almost as if we, as Christians, have 'superpowers' and 'supervictory'.

7. 'But thanks be to God, who gives us the victory through our Lord Jesus Christ' (1 Corinthians 15:57) (NKJV).

We have no reason not to be victorious in our daily battles and struggles. God, who is the all-sufficient one and all-powerful, lives inside of us through the Holy Spirit. We must live like victorious people and not give in to our weaknesses and battles. Prayer is the key to unlock that power.

> 8. 'But the Lord is faithful, who will establish you and guard you from the evil one' (2 Thessalonians 3:3) (NKJV).

The word 'guard' reminds us of military protection against attacks. That is the way God protects His children. God is faithful and will never allow us to be attacked if it is not going to strengthen our faith. God will give His angels instructions to protect us and, sometimes, these angels appear in human form and could be your next door neighbour or a friend. God works in mysterious ways His wonders to perform.

> 9 'Behold, I give you the authority to trample on serpents and scorpions, and over all the power of the enemy, and nothing shall by any means hurt you' (Luke 10:19) (NKJV).

Receiving the authority God refers to here does not mean that you should go out and look for serpents and scorpions to trample. God uses a metaphor to illustrate that whatever the form of the attack, we have the power to overcome it. We will not be left to fight the attacks alone with only ourselves to rely on. We will always have the help of the angels.

> 10 'Do not be overcome by evil, but overcome evil with good' (Romans 12:21) (NKJV).

As Christians, we should do the opposite when we are accused and bad-mouthed. We should not retaliate by doing what has been done to us. God expects us to represent Him here on earth, and in every situation we should ask ourselves: "What Would Jesus Do?" By doing so, we both protect ourselves and defend the image of God. We become stronger in doing what is right even when others do the wrong thing.

Chapter Eleven

Conclusion

God continued to bless us, in the natural and the super-natural aspects of our lives. Over the years in New Zealand, between 2008 and 2016, I studied and completed courses in several fields, obtaining numerous qualifications. I had the opportunity to work with youth from many different countries and cultures, globally. I was blessed in my series of temporary jobs, which had me working as a security training officer, a hospitality training officer, a hospitality manager, a head chef for a restaurant manager, and a housekeeping manager.

We started our journey from small beginnings and marvel at how God has brought us to where we are today. While we influence and impact youth globally, our reach is not limited to young people; through our service and ministry we affect larger communities of all ages, too. We had to endure and learn as we followed the course God set for us and our experiences contributed to our maturity. If God had not allowed all the things that happened to us in our lives, and had not guided us to the places we have visited, then I believe we could not speak about our experience of prophecy and our walk with God from a standpoint of authority.

Carol experienced the hand of God in her temporary career, from being a kindergarten teacher, then an Early Childhood Centre team leader to being the overseer of an Early Childhood Centre. Carol was blessed beyond measure. She is well-respected amongst the Pacific Island nations for her prayerful resilience and commitment. I have seen Carol mature from being a person dependent on me for everything to being a self-reliant individual who depends on God as her source of strength.

Candice is also blessed in that she received awards for excellence and commitment at a number of different schools she attended. She went on to be selected for the New Zealand Hip-Hop High School championships in Auckland. I have witnessed Candice maturing in prayer. She was always the shy girl amongst her friends, but in the last few years we have seen Candice come out of her shell and be more vocal in telling her friends about God and salvation. Candice completed a management qualification, by God's grace, and also continued studying Performing Arts. Candice is happily and successfully married to a great husband — a child of God and a family man, and their beautiful son, Raepheal, continues to thrive.

In the years between the prophecy he received and the fulfilment of his kingship, David was faithful to the promise of God, and led the people God gave him. So too, Carol and I embraced the prophecies in our lives and our purpose, and as we journey in the Spirit, we see God maturing our characters.

If we want to receive the blessings of God and do great things in the power of His spirit, then we must be willing to do the following:

1. Stand firm in God and in our beliefs. God has placed within us the power of choice. We can choose to obey God in everyday life

or we can choose to do our own thing and miss the blessings and suffer the consequences. Our choices we make will ultimately determine where we end up in life. Our attitude towards life is very important. We need to make the right choices with the right attitude. There is a saying: "Our attitude determines our altitude". If we approach life with a positive attitude, we will be amazed how high in life we can go. We can achieve great things.

2. See through the eyes of God. I remember reading a book when I was about fifteen, called *In His Steps: What Would Jesus Do?* by Charles M. Sheldon (originally published in 1896). In the book, we learn how the population of a town in the USA, starting with one church congregation, learns to live a Christian life and is transformed for God by seeing things the way God would see them — through His perspective. Their transformation becomes a catalyst that affects and changes the wider community and spreads its message into cities and churches that once seemed far beyond their reach. That is still so true today; when we see things from a different point of view, we can set change in motion. I have learnt to see things from God's perspective and that has changed my outlook on life.

3. Consider the old paths that others have travelled. Here we should not forget the people who have gone before us on our spiritual journey. Our parents and pastors are good sources of inspiration to us. I remember a pastor in our church in South Africa in 1990 (he sadly passed away in 2001), who encountered God, and we, as the youth back then, always looked up to that pastor. We would spend a lot of time with him to learn more about how he experienced God in a practical way.

4. Be willing to sacrifice some things. When we surrender to God and allow Him to control our lives, we are required to give up certain friends and let go of old habits. I remember I had a very close friend for over fifteen years, but when we started on this journey of prophecy, I had to let him go. It was difficult because we would go to the movies together, play sport together, and my mother liked him as if he was another one of her sons. My own family could not understand why I had to let him go but sacrifice is part of the journey we travel for God.

Like faith, prayer is very important in seeing prophecies come to pass. Daniel is known for his deep prayer-life. When he read the prophecy of Jeremiah revealing that the desolation of Israel would last for seventy years (Daniel 9:2), his response was not, "Oh well, I'll sit back, count the years, and the prophecy will automatically come to pass." Daniel knew that a lot had to happen for the prophecy to be fulfilled, and that time was short. The Bible records one of the things he did: 'So I turned to the Lord God and pleaded with him in prayer and petition, in fasting, and in sackcloth and ashes' (Daniel 9:3). We need to pray that what has been revealed in prophecy will come to pass.

Epilogue

YOUTH AFLAME INTERNATIONAL

God spoke to me in July 1993 and said that I should reach out to the youth of Paarl and ignite a spirit of unity. I was to **EMPOWER, EQUIP, ENGAGE, EDUCATE, EMBRACE, EMBARK, EXPERIENCE** to achieve my purpose in Christ.

The Youth Aflame organisation was founded on 23 October 1993 in Paarl, Western Cape, South Africa. Its major inaugural event sparked an infusion of members from various youth groups and later, Youth Aflame hosted several additional events including Peace Rally, 666-Musical outreach production, music festivals and youth camps.

The organisation branched out to the USA, Jamaica, Mexico, Canada, Australia, New Zealand, Pacific Islands, i.e. Fiji, Samoa and Tonga.

We will continue to empower the youth generation and prepare them for living in God's Kingdom.

H.P. Jakes Ministries

This ministry was founded in 2016 when I heard a word from God telling me that in order to reach leaders and impact nations, I needed to be organised and have structure in my life and activities. I thought about it and then realised that I needed to have a platform. This organisation should usher in the next phase of our journey. The ministry should be relevant and in today's challenging times, we need to provide services to the children of God beyond the boundaries of church walls. Jesus met the woman at the well and saved her. We, as a ministry, need to meet the sinner at the point of their need, the places where they meet with one another, and their places of employment. We should impact people just as Jesus impacted the world.

H.P. Jakes Ministries will embark on several community impact projects and annual Christian events that will include:

A. Community Impact Projects:

1. **Community Educare Centres,** where we will offer free kindergarten services to the community. Parents will be made co-owners of the concept and will contribute in the form of donations.

2. **Residential Care Centre for troubled, at-risk and addicted teens,** a place of healing and discovery. This will be a camp-like environment, where teens who are caught up in drugs and are having trouble at school and in society, will be invited to spend six months away from home, engage in skill-training, education,

rehabilitation and mentoring. This environment will allow them to 'discover themselves and their inner-champion'. They will engage with their parents after twelve weeks and start the healing process between them as a family.

3. **Community Home and Health Care,** a service to the most vulnerable of society, the elderly and disabled. We will offer services at their homes, assisting with home-care, personal-care and housekeeping.

B. Annual Christian-based Events:

1. **March – S.W.A.G (Saved With Amazing Grace) youth-leadership camps.** This will be held during the month of March every year, to empower and equip youth leaders and potential youth leaders, irrespective of race, creed, denomination and ethnicity.

2. **June/July – H.E.H.A. (Healthy Eating - Healthy Action) sports event.** This will be a family sports event, Olympic-style, to encourage healthy living and exercise. Teams from various churches and organisations will enter and represent a country of their choice. The day will start with a flag procession and the lighting of the torch. The torch will also represent the 'flame of life'. The spirit needs to reside in a healthy body. This event will assist in combatting obesity and diabetes and promoting better food choices.

3. **October – P-U-S-H Youth Conference (Persevere Until Success Happens).** This will be an annual, major youth conference,

hosting speakers from all over the world and impacting lives. The focus is on equipping and engaging people to live out a mission of relevance in the world today.

We continue to believe that God has called us for greatness.

**My life's motto: 'To fly with Eagles
- stop hanging out with Chickens'.**

Biography

Henry

MBA.(USA), B.Theol.(SA), Grad.Dip.Bus.Studs.(NZ), Dip.Mkt. Mgt.(SA), Cert.Mgt.Cons.(SA), Cert.Hos.(NZ), Cert.Bus.Mgt.(NZ).

Started his employment career as a chef in the South African Navy in 1985, served a six month stint in the SA Army, moved over to the South African Police Force, and worked with the South African Department of Correctional Services as a youth programme facilitator.

Started ministry at fourteen years of age, served as a drummer in the Anglican Church Lads' Brigade marching band, was a Sunday-school teacher at sixteen, youth leader at eighteen, youth pastor at twenty-five, pastor at twenty-six, and Youth Aflame president at the age of thirty.

He has studied relentlessly while he was working and obtained a Master's degree, a Bachelor's degree, two post-graduate diplomas, two national diplomas, and ten certificates in various fields.

The following are his areas of expertise: policing, security, hospitality, project management, manufacturing, education and training, youth and community development, chef and catering, business owner, hotel management, housekeeping management, and pastoring.

Won numerous awards including: Community Policing Officer of the Year in Wellington, South Africa in 1998; and finalist for the Western Cape Police Officer of the Year award. Also achieved numerous police commendations and citations. Featured on Radio Pulpit in 1997, Radio-KC in 1998, and SABC 2's Pasella programme in 2000 and 2016 (Encore).

Carol

Dip.Ed.(SA), Dip.ECE.(NZ)

Carol started her career teaching special needs children in 1990, then taught deaf children and autistic children, and taught rural kindergarten in three countries. After thirty years in teaching, she went on to do housekeeping and now community health care, working with the elderly and the disabled.

Carol won numerous awards and citations for outstanding work as a teacher:

- In 2003, the Teacher of the Year at Klapmuts Primary School, Western Cape, South Africa.
- In 2004, finalist for the Face2Face, SABC TV programme's Make-Over show.

- In 2006, Teacher of the Year award at L.B. Yancey Elementary School, Henderson, Vance County, North Carolina, USA.
- In 2006, VIF Program team leader for foreign teachers travelling to the USA.
- In 2010, early childhood teacher team leader and in charge of the McKenzie House Early Childhood Centre in Carterton, New Zealand.

www.ingramcontent.com/pod-product-compliance
Lightning Source LLC
Chambersburg PA
CBHW071355290426
44108CB00014B/1562